MW00570826

straight answers

for Kids about Life, God, and Growing Up

by
William L. Coleman

Illustrated by Michael Boze

Chariot Books™
David C. Cook Publishing Co.

Chariot Books™ is an imprint of David C. Cook Publishing Co.
David C. Cook Publishing Co., Elgin, IL 60120
David C. Cook Publishing Co., Weston, Ontario
Nova Distributors, Ltd., Torquay, England

STRAIGHT ANSWERS FOR KIDS ABOUT LIFE, GOD, AND GROWING UP

Edited by Jeannie Harmon
Designed and illustrated by Michael Boze

First printing, 1992
Printed in the United States of America
96 95 94 93 92 5 4 3 2 1

*All Scripture quotations in this publication unless otherwise noted are from the Holy Bible, New
International Version. Copyright © 1973, 1978, 1984, International Bible Society.*

Library of Congress Cataloging-in-Publication Data
Coleman, William L.
     Straight answers for kids about life, God, and growing up / by William L. Coleman ;
illustrated by Michael Boze.
     p. cm.
     Summary: Provides answers to questions young Christians have about family matters,
personal pressures, school problems, body development, drugs, sex, and God. Features related
Bible verses.
     ISBN 1-55513-336-3   .
     1. Children—Religious life.   2. Christian life—1960—Juvenile literature.   [1. Conduct of
life,   2. Christian life.]   I. Boze, Michael, ill.   II. Title.
BV4571.2.C585   1992
248.8'2—dc20
                                                                                                    91-41504
                                                                                                         CIP
                                                                                                          AC

Dedicated to the kids of the
Harvard Evangelical Free Church

Table of Contents

Getting in Touch with My Family

Parents Are Good, but Sometimes 9

Brothers and Sisters Drive You Bonkers 13

The Mystery of Divorce 17

Stepparents Can Be Cool 22

Empty Homes After School 26

Getting in Touch with Myself and My Friends

Feeling Out of It 31

Left Out of the Party 34

When Your Friends Do You Dirty 37

Lying, Cheating and Stealing 40

Sometimes Teasing Hurts 44

Prejudice Is Painful 48

Saying Yes and No 53

Strange and Evil Thoughts 55

Young Stress 57

Someone To Talk To 62

The Alcohol Problem 65

What Are Drugs Like? 68

Getting in Touch with School

Getting Along with Teachers 72

Sports Pressure 76

How Important Are Grades 80

Getting in Touch with My Sexuality

Awkward Boys 84
Growing Girls 86
What Is Love? 88
Why Wait to Have Sex? 90
The AIDS Problem 92
Could We Be Homosexual? 95
Is the Good Feeling Really Bad? 97

Getting in Touch with Difficult Things in My Life

What Is Death Like? 101
When Serious Illness Comes 107
The Miserable Life of Runaways 109

Getting in Touch with God

What Is God Like? 112
Am I A Christian? 118
Talking to God 121

Getting in Touch with the Future

Future World 125

it's a crazy world . . .

One day your best friend isn't talking to you and the next day your body starts to change. On Tuesday you get invited to a party and on Thursday you hear about a neighbor who has AIDS. It's a crazy world.

In the morning you see a student cheat on a test. By afternoon someone is passing a magazine around the locker room. It's a crazy world.

When things change so fast, you have a hundred questions. In this book you will find over 350 of those questions and their answers. I hope they will help you make each day a great adventure.

Bill Coleman
Aurora, Nebraska

getting in touch with my family

my parents are good, but sometimes . . .

You should see my parents. They dress right out of the sixties. How can I get them to change? I'm embarrassed to go anywhere with them.

Don't try to change your parents. Learn to love them as they are.

You might buy a modern necktie for your dad's birthday or a neat scarf for Mom, but don't try any major overhauls. Besides, if your parents keep their clothes, that style might come back someday. Remember, too, that you might look just as strange to them.

Be proud of your parents. There is much more to them than the latest fashion fad.

And parents are the pride of their children.
Proverbs 17:6b

My dad tells the corniest jokes anybody ever heard. Can't somebody tell him to knock it off, especially when my friends are over?

Most children seem to feel uptight when their parents try to joke around their friends. And maybe some children take it too seriously. So what if his jokes fall flat. Your friends understand; they have fathers, too.

The best advice is to let Dad be Dad. But if you are convinced that he is a comedic disaster, say something to Mom. She may have a way of calming him down.

How do I tell my parents that watching television won't rot my brain or make me a murderer?

Just the way you said it. Then, after you've said this, show them you can lead a normal life with plenty of well-rounded activities. If you're a living room lizard

You should see my parents. They dress right out of the sixties

and you spend every waking hour drooling in your potato chips bag, it's hard to believe you're leading a full life.

My dad travels all the time, and I hardly ever get to see him. If I ask him, do you think he would stay home more or get another job?

I know how to find out. Ask him. Some dads and moms may not be able to get a job close to home, but some may. Let your dad know how much he means to you. That might get him to thinking. Tell him you would be happy with less money and more dad. He should feel like a million bucks to know how much he means to you.

Staying home more may not be possible for your dad. If this is the case, talk to him about making better use of the time he has at home. Perhaps suggest that he set aside a time when just the two of you can be together— go out for ice cream or pizza, or go to a ball game.

None of my friends pray before they eat at their house. How can I get my parents to stop doing this, especially when we have company?

A recent report says that half of the families in the United States still pray before eating at least one meal at home. Families don't have to do it, but why knock it? Chill out!

Children, obey your parents in the Lord, for this is right.
Ephesians 6:1

My parents always drag me along to Grandmother's house. It is really boring. Can't they leave me home?

Look for a more constructive solution. Is there something you would like to do in connection with your trip to Grandmother's? Stop at a ballpark, a playground, a lake? Pick up Grandmother at her house and take her somewhere? Can you bring a friend along?

Some dads didn't grow up with compliments at home and have trouble learning to give them. Often they need a child to teach them.

Also remember that being a family requires that everyone needs to give as well as take. You might consider helping your grandmother as your contribution to the well-being of your family. Who knows? You might end up enjoying yourself in the process.

I think I'd fall down if my dad ever said anything nice to me. I feel like a baby asking him for compliments.

Give your dad a good example. Compliment him. Tell him you like his clothes or his car or his lawn or whatever it is he does. Leave a note on his dresser or stuff it in his shoe.

Some dads didn't grow up with compliments at home and have trouble learning to give them. Often they need a child to teach them. Children are master teachers.

Someone should tell my parents that video games can actually make you think better.

If that's true, your next report card should show how much better you are thinking.

My dad makes fun of me at the dinner table. Sometimes I want to cry. What should I do?

One thing is to let your dad know how much it hurts. It may not be easy but you might need to tell him. Keep it short and direct. Tell him you feel bad when he makes fun of you. He may not be aware of what is happening. Your dad might think you are enjoying this along with him.

If you think it would be dangerous to say this to your dad, you could talk it over with your mother first.

When I am alone with my father he sits close and touches me where I don't like it. How can I make him stop?

Tell your mother immediately. Don't stop to think it over. Don't try to figure it

My dad travels all the time and I hardly ever get to see him.

don't judge a parent when he is having a bad day.

out. Tell your mother today. If for some reason you can't tell your mother, tell some adult—a relative, Sunday school teacher, school teacher, etc.

Avoid being alone with him. If this isn't always possible, don't ever be afraid to say "no" if you start feeling uncomfortable about his advances.

I don't think my parents are glad they had children.

Some days the work, the pressure, the finances get to parents and they have second thoughts. But don't judge a parent when he is having a bad day. Most of the time parents are proud and excited that they have their children.

brothers and sisters drive you bonkers

Why do sisters talk so much? I hate to go anywhere with our family because my sister is always yapping.

Be thankful you don't have to be responsible for how other people behave. Enjoy talking at your own pace and let your sister rattle on.

As she gets older she might talk less—and then again she could talk more.

My brother hits me. Should I tell my mother?

Definitely. Physical fights are dangerous. Hitting should be off limits. It's painful, dominating, and terribly unfair.

My brother is always correcting me. No matter what I say, he says I'm wrong. Shouldn't my parents stop him?

They could, and if he does it a lot in public, they should tell him to put a lock on it. But that won't stop him from doing it in private. You may have to wait until he grows up a little before that comes to an end. Meanwhile, look at it as a stage he has to grow out of, and he will when he feels more sure of himself.

What do you do if your sister keeps taking your stuff without asking?

Do you take her stuff without asking? I find a lot of sisters think they should be able to borrow a top anytime they want, but they expect their sisters to always ask.

Make some ground rules. Explain what she can borrow without asking if she returns it. Describe exactly what she *always* must ask about before she can use it. Then ask her to give you the same guidelines about her stuff. It goes better if both of you have the same set of rules.

My brother hits me. Should I tell my mother?

My brother keeps getting into trouble at school and my friends tease me about it. It doesn't do any good to tell him to knock it off, either.

Your situation is painful. But there are some steps you can take to ease the problem:

1. Don't feel sorry for yourself. All of us have trouble. Pouting makes it worse.
2. Hold your head up straight. You are a person and you have nothing to be ashamed of.
3. Make your own mark. The way you live tells more about you than your brother's behavior can reflect on you.

You can't change others but you can control yourself. Ask God to help you keep your attitudes in check and then stand on your own two feet.

I have an older brother who won't stop calling me names. I call him names back but he just keeps it up.

Calling people names usually causes them to yell more names back. Ignoring him is probably the best action. When you get upset or retaliate, he is spurred on to call you more in return. His goal may be to get you to blow your stack, and it sounds like he's getting what he wants.

This may sound crazy, but my brother gets a lot more for birthdays and Christmas than I do.

Most of the time we imagine that our brother or sister gets more than we do, but sometimes it's true. If this is what's happening with you, your parents should be able to clear up the problem.

First, make sure you aren't adding the facts wrong. Second, if you are still convinced the problem exists, ask your parents about it. Be sure and say this kindly. Don't accuse them of doing something sneaky or underhanded.

Try this: "This may be my imagination but it looks like my brother is getting a lot better stuff than I get. Am I just dreaming?"

Calling people names usually causes them to yell more names back. Ignoring him is probably the best action.

You won't be the first child to ask this of his parents, and you'll probably come away with a good answer.

What do you do if your sister likes to watch a television show at the same time football is on?

You work out a deal. If left alone children are often very good at solving problems for themselves. I have a great deal of confidence that you two can swap some shows, trade chores, or do something that will make both of you reasonably happy.

Then he threw his arms around his brother Benjamin
and wept, and Benjamin embraced him, weeping.
Genesis 45:14

Our parents are divorced, and I don't get to see my sister very often. I barely know her.

Is the problem the distance between your parents' houses or do your parents simply not get along or what? Try to figure out what is happening. Ask them why the visits are so infrequent. Just by asking you may cause the situation to improve. Make some suggestions as to how your parents might be able to get you together.

Also let your sister know how much you want to get together. That might make her work harder to push things from her side.

What would you do if you told your sister a secret, and she told it to somebody else?

Confront her. Tell her that you can't trust her until she proves herself to you. The burden of proof here is with your sister. Then if she continues to betray your trust, don't tell her any more secrets.

What do you do if your sister likes to watch a television show at the same time football is on?

If you react and get angry, it may encourage him to keep on teasing. Don't feed his habit.

My brother teases me all the time and I hate it.

Some of the meanest teasing goes on between brothers and sisters. Too often it isn't meant to be fun but is done only to ridicule and put down the other person. If there is tension between the two, they are better off joking about objects or events and not about each other.

Remember, if you react and get angry, it may encourage him to keep on teasing. Don't feed his habit. Briefly say why you don't like his teasing and walk away.

I tell my brother to knock before he comes into my room, but he never does.

Do you knock when you go into his room? Talk to your parents and see if they can do something about the problem first. You might suggest that you need a lock for your door.

the mystery of divorce

I'm working on this deal where I can get my parents back together. Any suggestions on what I should do?

Getting them back together sounds like a great idea. Most children want to see their parents together and living in the same house. But if they are already divorced, your odds are very, very poor. Generally speaking, people who have ended their marriage do not marry each other again.

I don't like to ruin dreams so I won't say don't try. But you need to know it seldom happens.

The best thing to do is to pray for your parents that God would help them through this tough time. And then try to love each parent as he or she is. More than anything else right now they need your support.

My dad and I didn't get along very well. I think that had a lot to do with the reason why he left.

It's hard to say why your parents split up. Maybe they aren't even sure what caused the divorce. Whatever the reason, it is between your parents. They alone are responsible for that choice. Many kids feel responsible for the divorce of their parents, but kids don't make decisions for their parents. Parents are responsible for their own actions.

My dad left almost a year ago. He's been to see me only twice since then. I'd like to get together more often.

Tell your dad that. Phone him, write him, whatever it takes. He might imagine that you don't want to see him. He might think you are too busy. Don't let your dad guess how you feel.

I'm working on this deal where I can get my parents back together.

I live with my dad, but I really want to live with my mother.

I realize that you probably didn't have a choice as to where you would live. You may not have the option to change even now. If you do, consider these things before making any big changes:

1. Be cautious! Why do you want to move? Do you think life will be better at your mom's house? Maybe things will only be different. She might let you do some things but she could be stricter about others.
2. Be specific! Know exactly why you want to make the move. Write it down and ask yourself if it's true.
3. Look for a compromise. Can you accomplish the same thing by staying with your father and spending more time with your mother?

It's a big move. Be sure you have thought it through before you ask for the switch. Trying to switch back later can be painful.

Every day my mother criticizes my father. I get tired of it. My dad has lots of good qualities, too. I don't know what to say to her.

You don't need to defend your father or his actions. That's his problem. If your mother isn't open to hearing good things about her former husband, don't force them on her. By sticking up for him you may cause her to dump on him all the more.

Sometimes without thinking about it, parents look to their children as a substitute for a counselor or friend. Your mom needs to release some of the hurt she's experiencing, and she feels you can be trusted with the information. Without agreeing with her you might say something like, "You have a lot of pain, don't you?" or "I'm sorry you hurt so much."

When you can, gently change the subject. You shouldn't have to listen to all of it, but at the same time she is looking for someone to unload on.

My dad says he loves me and misses me. Why doesn't he come to see me?

As for your father, you have to judge his behavior for yourself. If the two of you can have a fair, caring relationship, then by all means go for it, even if your mother's experience has not been very good.

If God hates divorce, doesn't he hate my parents for getting divorced?

God wants us to have a satisfying and happy marriage. He wishes we would stay together and work things out. Certainly God is opposed to divorce. Most of us are opposed to divorce. It causes a tremendous amount of pain for everyone. But that doesn't mean God hates the people who get divorced. He loves your parents just as much today as He did before the divorce.

My dad says he loves me and misses me. Why doesn't he come to see me?

Ask your father that exact question. No one can answer for him, and it sounds like he owes you an explanation. Try to remember that even though parents love their kids, they sometimes don't stop long enough to ask their children how they feel. By talking to your dad, he might come to realize his need to be a bigger part of your life.

A television show says the children of divorce grow up to get divorced themselves. Am I going to get divorced?

If your father is a mechanic, does that mean you will be a mechanic? If your mother is a cub scout leader, does that mean you have to become a cub scout leader?

You are a person. You make decisions on your own. When and if you get married, you can put all of your love and caring and strength into that marriage.

You have great potential for a fantastic marriage.

(If you believe all the statistics you hear, you are also supposed to have 2.3 children — and that's hard to do.)

If your mother isn't open to hearing good things about her former husband, don't force them on her.

If you are willing to try and forgive, you might be able to rebuild a relationship with your dad. If you choose to stay angry, you will feel like you are at war with him.

We don't have much money and my dad doesn't send his support check. I wonder if it would help if I wrote him a note and told him how broke we are.

Probably not. Finances and support are adult business. It affects children but the collecting is for parents to work out.

You may not have all the facts. You don't know what has been agreed on. If you're not careful, you could be used by one parent to get even with the other.

As much as the lack of money hurts, you better let someone else do the dealing.

I thought my parents could work things out, but then my dad walked out on us. I'm really angry at him.

Go ahead and be angry. It's not wrong to be angry. Your life has been seriously disrupted, and you are left hurt and bewildered. That's enough to make anyone angry.

Now ask yourself what you are going to do with your anger. Some people are furious for the rest of their lives. You can control your anger, and the sooner you deal with it the better things will go for you and everyone else.

The next step is forgiveness. If you are willing to try and forgive, you might be able to rebuild a relationship with your dad. If you choose to stay angry, you will feel like you are at war with him. The earlier you are able to forgive the easier it will be.

Get rid of all bitterness, rage and anger, brawling and slander, along with every form of malice. Be kind and compassionate to one another, forgiving each other, just as in Christ God forgave you.
Ephesians 4:31, 32

My dad left my mom and me and now the church has made her give up her Sunday school class. Is that fair?

Sometimes people want to help keep marriages together and they do things that are confusing. Maybe the leaders in your church will realize how much your mother can help her Sunday School class and let her teach again.

When I visit my dad he never tells me what to do. But when I'm at home, my mom is always griping about something. Can't somebody tell her to give it a rest?

Sounds like you have a "holiday" dad. You don't visit often and when you do, he makes it a party. I can't defend your mother, but she may be facing a harder job. My guess is she has less money and she needs to make tough decisions like setting down rules and getting you to do things.

Before you judge, you might ask what kind of a load she has to pull.

After our dad left, my mom said that since I am the oldest, I will have to be the dad around here. I don't think I'm ready to be a father.

Your mother sounds frustrated and wants to lean on someone for help. Pitch in with more help, but don't try to be a dad. Volunteer for more jobs around the house, keep an eye on the other children, and tell your mother she's great.

With an important person missing, more is expected from everyone. Give more of yourself and stay a child at the same time.

My parents have divorced but no one tells me why. Don't I have a right to know?

Yes, you deserve an explanation. But you may not need to know all of the details. Some things are their private business.

You deserve an honest answer. They should not make up lies to try and "protect" you.

Don't be surprised if the answer is a simple, "We don't love each other anymore." Whatever it is, you should be given some information as to why your life is being tossed around.

After our dad left, my mom said that since I am the oldest, I will have to be the dad around here.

stepparents can be cool

My mother is dating a guy and I want to know if this is serious.

You bet you do and you have a right to know what is happening. Not that the details are any of your business, but you need to be informed about their intentions.

Tell your mother how you feel. Ask her to keep you posted on developments. If they're talking marriage, you want to get to know this person a little bit at a time. You need time to get acquainted and build a relationship.

The decision to marry or not to marry is your mother's to make, but she would be smart to bring you into the picture as soon as possible. You shouldn't be "shocked" and find out suddenly that they plan to tie the knot.

Step number one is to let her know you are interested. Ask polite questions about him. Get into a conversation with him when he comes over. Make a great attempt at getting along and most likely you will.

I have a stepmother and she drives me nuts.

Be specific; that's too broad. Describe what it is about her that gives your brain pain.

If you want to help solve a problem, you need to begin by explaining exactly what it is that sends you up the wall.

My mother is seeing this man and I feel like I'm being dumped.

Often people in love lose all ability to think straight, and this could be happening to your mother. Be patient with her but also try to call her back to reality. There are several things you might say to your mother in a direct, loving way:

1. I'm happy for your new relationship, but I hope you and I can stay close, too.
2. When you go out on a date, I feel better if I know what time you might

My mother is seeing this man and I feel like I'm being dumped.

come home. (Children worry just like parents worry.)

3. I'm glad you are going on a date Friday night; could you and I do something Saturday?

It takes maturity to solve problems with your parents, but many children can do it with straight-love talk. Maybe your mother thinks you are glad she goes away so much. Keep her informed about how you feel.

My dad wants me to call my stepmother "Mom." I already have a mom.

When my dad remarried, I was an older teenager and he asked me to call his new bride "Mom." For me that was asking too much and I never did.

It is important that everyone reaches an agreement on what to call each other. If an agreement isn't reached, you may end up not calling each other anything.

Tell your biological parent how you feel about calling your stepmother "Mom." If possible, suggest some other names you might use including her first name. You may have to compromise, but you can do that. It might be best if the three of you sit down and discuss this together. After you have known one another for a while you might change what you call each other. You can expect your relationship to grow.

You might ask your stepmother how she would like to be addressed. Something like, "I already call my mother 'Mom'; what name would you be comfortable with?" At the same time tell her what name you enjoy being called.

How should I introduce my stepmother to my friends?

That depends on what you have agreed to call your stepmother. Remember, neither your friends nor their parents need an explanation of who she is each time you meet. Make it simple and natural.

Maybe it will be: "Mom," "Mother," "My stepmother," "Linda" or whatever her first name is, or "Linda, my stepmother."

It takes maturity to solve problems with your parents, but many children can do it with straight-love talk.

I don't think my stepfather should tell me what to do. I lived here first.

This is one of the toughest problems for kids with stepparents. Who is in charge of discipline and who can tell whom to do what? Who lays down the rules and who enforces them?

Family conferences or powwows or table talks become helpful in working out the rules. As much as possible, a family needs to decide on curfews and chores and duties together. They also need to agree on what the consequences are if anyone fails to keep those rules.

When families join together in establishing the guidelines, they often cooperate better in keeping those rules. Cooperation takes the pressure off and there is less need to have one or two people telling everyone what to do.

However, your stepparent will probably feel more strongly about some rules than you feel. Give yourselves plenty of time to become acquainted, and you may find you agree with each other more and more.

So far, so good—my stepfather acts like Santa Claus. He gives me anything I want.

For your sake I hope that doesn't last too long. At first some stepparents roll in with lots of presents. They take you out for milk shakes every fifteen minutes, rub your hair around, and buy you electronic toys. They want you to like them. That part is good.

What they need to do is calm down and let friendship come naturally. If they try to buy your friendship, what will happen when the presents end? Tell your stepfather he doesn't have to buy you things, even if it hurts you to say it. Suggest you do things that are free, like play catch, paint a model, fly kites, play a video game, take a hike.

Spend time together and get to know each other. Your friendship will last much longer than the presents.

My stepfather acts like Santa Claus. He gives me anything I want.

I used to get a lot of attention before this man came along. I don't think my mother loves me as much as she used to.

This seems like a common feeling, especially if a child and a single parent have spent months or years with just the two together. As with most problems, tell your mother what your fear is.

Love is not a fossil fuel like coal or gas. We don't burn it up until it's all gone. Love is more like a garden. If we keep planting flowers and vegetables, there will be plenty to go around.

Your mother has a garden filled with love. Stay close to her and you can keep getting baskets full.

I'm about to get a stepbrother and a stepsister. I don't need this kind of aggravation.

Most new families are tricky business. Keep your cool; they probably feel the same about you. If you give the situation some of your best personality, you might charm everyone into getting along fairly well.

For guidelines, try to keep these two balls juggling in the air all the time:

1. Look for interests to share. You don't have to compete or beat them at everything. Just look for things to do together.
2. Keep your individuality. A room of your own or an area where you can store your "stuff" will make you feel like a person. You have a need to be you. Don't get lost in the shuffle or "blended" family.

Love is not a fossil fuel like coal or gas. We don't burn it up until it's all gone.

empty homes after school

My parents work and I have to come home after school. I'm afraid to be alone.

Tell your parents that today. Explain exactly what bothers you about it and insist that they help you. There are steps which can take most of the worry out of coming home alone. You deserve help with this.

I'd like to find someplace to go after school. My house is empty and I don't like to be there.

First talk to your parents about creative places where you could spend an hour or two safely.

The local library is usually a good place between three and five o'clock. You can get your homework done and be free to do other things all evening at home.

A safe playground will allow you to have fun and kill an hour with your friends. Some churches have developed programs after school.

Whatever you decide, make sure your parents know where you are going to be.

My parents don't want me tying up the phone after school, but I have no one to talk to.

My parents don't want me tying up the phone after school, but I have no one to talk to.

If there are no people around, the phone can be helpful if it is controlled. Naturally that means no calls that charge money or where you can order merchandise.

Ask your parents if you can make three 5-minute phone calls. Space them out over the time you are alone. One call to your parents (that will be brief). A second call to a friend. A third call to a special person. Some areas have volunteers who are available to talk to young people who are home alone. Ask your teacher if such a line exists. These phone friends might help with homework; they might give counseling; maybe they are just available to chat. (Make sure your parents approve any place you call for advice.)

If your parents were convinced you could control how much you use the phone, they might be willing to let you use it more. Give it your best shot.

What's the big deal about an empty house after school? I love it.

It depends a lot on the person and the situation. Often a young person looks forward to running his own life for a couple of hours.

Joey comes over after school and smokes in my basement. He won't stop even though I told him I don't like it.

Next time don't let Joey in the house. Be just that direct. Tell him he can't come in your house until he promises not to smoke. Tell your parents immediately.

You are running at least two risks. One, you could burn the house down. Two, he could pick up a terrible habit and put your health in danger. Second-hand smoke is dangerous for you, too. Cigarette smoking and drinking alcohol are two of the greatest problems young people face after school.

Take a strong stand and Joey will probably respect you for it. If you lose Joey's friendship, that's a chance you have to take.

Am I a slave or what? I shouldn't have to cook supper after I get home from school.

Slow down. Are you cooking the entire supper or just getting it started? All of the meal might be too much, but what's wrong with making the salad or pudding? Talk to your mother about helping out, but don't give her your slave speech.

Cigarette smoking and drinking alcohol are two of the greatest problems young people face after school.

My mother wants me to take out the trash, pick up the living room, and feed the cats after school. What can I do?

Take out the trash, pick up the living room and feed the cats.

When people call, I'm not supposed to say my mother and father are working. Isn't that lying?

Tell the caller your mother or father can't come to the phone now. That's a fact.

I asked my parents to give me a list of the most important things in the house in case there is a fire. I want to know what to save first.

You are the most important thing in the house. Save yourself.

It's boring to just sit and watch television after school.

Here are some suggestions:

1. Get an early start on your homework.
2. Surprise your mom by doing something special for her—make her a card, do an additional chore, etc.
3. Learn to play an instrument at school and practice at home.
4. Take up a new hobby. There are several how-to videos at the local library. Do a little research and learn a new skill.
5. Talk to your pastor. Name five or six children your age who are just as bored and tell him you would like something to do. He might be able to come up with the activity you are looking for.

If his eyes don't light up immediately, add this bit of information: according to a report by the National Institute on Drug Abuse, "latchkey" kids are more likely to use drugs than those with parents at home. Tell him you want to head off a problem before it begins.

I wish my mom would quit her job and stay home more with us kids.

Your mom needs to hear what you think and how you feel. Then you need to listen to how she thinks and how she feels. Do you understand what drives her toward a job? Does she understand why you want to keep her home?

After you both have said how you feel, move toward action. What could each of you do to help each other?

My guess is that this conversation could result in an even greater love and closeness between the two of you.

I hear all of this complaining about working mothers, but I'm kind of proud that my mother works.

Many children are. She would love to hear that.

It's no fun having your twelve-year-old sister in charge. I'm ten years old and I can take care of myself.

You might be able to. Remember I said "might." Discuss this with your parents. Ask if each of you can be in charge of yourself. Often a "boss" relationship works poorly among children.

I'm nine and I'm scared to stay home alone.

You are too young to be left by yourself. Ask your mother or father if you can stay with a neighbor.

Sometimes my mom gets home at five o'clock and the next time it's seven o'clock. It seems too long to wait.

Maybe your mom can't do anything about it, but at least mention your problem. Ask her to come straight home and then you can shop for groceries together if necessary.

If she is going to be late, ask her to give you a call. Children worry about their parents just like parents worry about their children.

It's no fun having your twelve-year-old sister in charge.

getting in touch with myself and my friends

feeling out of it

I'm afraid I really am a nerd, and sometimes I wish I could be someone else.

If you aren't happy with who you seem to be, why not change your appearance or change a behavior you don't like about yourself, such as having a quick temper, not showing kindness, or always losing things? Don't change it for others, but you don't sound happy with your life-style.

There are some things none of us can change. I'm not going to become a star basketball player. Believe me, I've tried. That's accepting reality.

But if you don't want to be a nerd, stop looking and acting like one. Stop carrying pencils in your shirt pocket. Get a stylish haircut. Mix with a wider spectrum of people. Don't be a recluse.

You may not want to chase every fad and join every clique in school, but don't live in a laboratory beaker either. Air yourself out and get to know a variety of friends.

Aren't some people more naturally shy?

Most of us are shy. Even actors, politicians, ministers, and hot dog salespeople are sometimes shy people, but they have decided to fight their shyness and become more outgoing.

It's hard to say how we became shy, but we do know most of us can overcome it. Don't hide under the staircase and play with spiderwebs. We fight shyness by practicing. Meet people. Look them in the eye and talk. You will find your shyness less painful with experience.

I don't have much energy. School seems dull, and I don't enjoy doing anything.

Frankly, some people like a dull and boring life. Someone could make suggestions all day and they wouldn't pull themselves out of it. You must not be one of those or you wouldn't have asked.

Aren't some people more naturally shy?

A few ideas:

1. Get your eyes off yourself. Who is less fortunate than you? How can you help them? Read to a blind person, help someone in a wheelchair around the school. We all need purpose.
2. Find a hobby you secretly want to try—karate club, journalism, underwater yodeling, whatever. Look for good action.
3. Get some exercise. Wake up those corpuscles and get them chasing each other around your system. Work out or join an aerobics class.
4. If you are sure none of these will help, see a doctor. You could be low on something.

Finally, brothers, whatever is true, whatever is noble, whatever is right, whatever is pure, whatever is lovely, whatever is admirable—if anything is excellent or praiseworthy—think about such things.
Philippians 4:8

Every once in a while I get down and can't seem to feel better.

Every once in a while I get down and can't seem to feel better.

Ask yourself what has brought you out of the dumps in the past. Obviously you didn't stay there forever, so what changed your mood? Does a movie help perk you up? Does a phone call to a friend bring you back to reality? Some people go outside and play with their dogs.

We usually have three or four activities that are almost guaranteed to alter our moods. The problem is we either forget what they are or we refuse to use them. Mood changers don't have to be powerful like alcohol or drugs. For most of us they are simple and manageable, like friends, recreation, or some new scenery.

It's easy to get down. How long we stay down is often a choice we make.

Lisa is a grouch, and her attitude makes me feel blue half the time.

There is no doubt that our friends affect us. If we hang around cheery people, we tend to be up, and if we rub elbows with a grump, our jowls start to sag. In some cases a few short sentences might help change your friend. Try some gems like:

You sure are grumpy a lot.

Hey, lighten up.

You are a lot better looking when you smile.

She may not be aware that she has become such a shrivel face.

Mood changers don't have to be powerful like alcohol or drugs. For most of us they are simple and manageable, like friends, recreation, or some new scenery.

left out of the party

I'm not as popular as my friends. Is there anything I can do to become more popular?

Collecting a large number of acquaintances or getting invited to a list of places isn't a high priority on my list of goals. Being a good friend is important. Aim to be a first-class friend. Be a good listener. Share yourself. Be available. Laugh and enjoy. Help when you can. Keep secrets.

Do all of these things and you still might not be high on the popularity chart, but you'll get to know a few people who will mean something special to you.

There seem to be plenty of parties going on, and I don't get invited.

Throw a party of your own and invite six people. Also be sure to invite yourself.

Everybody likes Sonja, but I don't seem to be on her level.

If your goal is to be like Sonja, you will get eaten up by jealousy and envy. Be you. Be a great you. Be the best you can be.

The world is full of people who want to be like someone else. They're miserable because they can never reach that goal. If your target is to be a great you, you have a terrific chance of hitting the center.

Laura has invited me to every party she has ever had. This year she didn't invite me to her birthday party. Don't you think I should ask her about that?

Probably not. Have you noticed a change in her behavior toward you otherwise? If not, drop it. She may have simply forgotten to ask you. On the other hand, Laura possibly wanted to have one party without you. Why not?

If she still treats you the same, I would swallow hard and forget it.

Andy and Kevin are both my friends, but Andy can't stand Kevin.

Andy and Kevin are both my friends, but Andy can't stand Kevin. Should I stop seeing Kevin?

By no means. Our friends often don't quite fit with each other. Don't plan things that force Andy and Kevin to be together, but be friends with both.

My friend doesn't go to church at all. A girl in my Sunday school class says I shouldn't hang around with non-Christians.

Ask yourself a few questions:

Is she causing you to do things you shouldn't?

Is she tearing your faith apart?

Is she pulling you away from Christians?

If the answer is no to all of these, I'd stick with her. You might be able to show her what Christ means to you.

At school there seems to be the insiders and the outsiders. If you have money and you are a big shot, you fit into the insiders. It really makes you feel bad if you're left out.

That's a terrible feeling. If you let that "left out" feeling get to you, you could turn bitter. This might not help, but give it a try: "Any group that excludes you because you don't have enough money isn't worth belonging to."

That's true whether you are in the fifth grade, the eleventh grade, college, or the business world. People are valuable because they are made in the image of God, no matter if they are rich or poor. God loves the beggar as much as He loves the president of any club. He doesn't love the beggar more but certainly the same.

There is nothing wrong with having money, but there is something very wrong with saying that people with money are somehow better than people who don't have money.

Anyone who leaves you out because you aren't rich is a person who doesn't quite understand what makes a person worthwhile.

People are valuable because they are made in the image of God, no matter if they are rich or poor.

So in everything, do to others what you would have them do to you.
Matthew 7:12a

The youth group at my church does a lot of things, but I feel like they're a clique or whatever. I feel like saying something to the youth sponsor.

A fantastic idea. Do it right away. Cliques would be a great subject for discussion at one of your meetings. Some youth groups invite anybody and everybody in. Others have a narrow, tight concept of whom to accept.

Pick up the phone and call the sponsor.

When I hang out with my friends, I often end up doing things I know I wouldn't do if I were by myself. I don't know if that should bother me or not.

That depends on what you are doing. Sometimes friends can get you to improve your behavior. But that doesn't sound like the problem you have in mind.

Write this on the back of your hand: "A pack mentality can get you into trouble."

If you let the group do your thinking for you, it's easier to end up doing stupid things. Hold on to your own brain. Ask God to give you the courage to turn down the pack when you know you ought to.

Brad is in a wheelchair and I want to invite him to our party. Lisa says no, because he'd get in the way. Shouldn't we ask him anyway?

That depends. If you can invite Brad as a friend or as someone you would like to get to know, give him a shot.

But if you want to invite Brad because you feel sorry for him, you better think it over. A pity party for Brad is bound to be a loser. Don't start a rent-the-handicapped program. If you are ready to make him part of the party, call his number.

If you let the group do your thinking for you, it's easier to end up doing stupid things. Hold on to your own brain.

when your friends do you dirty

I have this close friend and we do neat things together. The only thing is that she lies. I don't know if I should just ignore her lying or what.

Some people can. I know a few people who are notorious liars and their close friends seem to put up with it. That doesn't seem to add up. The formula should go like this: Truth = Trust = Friendship.

The opposite formula is: Lying = Distrust = Suspicion. It's hard to be a close friend with someone you distrust. Tell your friend she is loose with the truth and that it bothers you. If she doesn't improve, you might want to slide away.

Lisa has a terrible temper. If she throws a fit, she's likely to break things. My mom says I should drop her.

Listen to your mother.

> *Do not make friends with a hot-tempered man,*
> *do not associate with one easily angered.*
> Proverbs 22:24

What do you say to a person who keeps taking your things?

How about "Good-bye"?

I have this close friend and we do neat things together. The only thing is that she lies.

37

Suzanne is a good friend but she never wants to do the things I want. I get tired of just doing her stuff all the time.

It's no fun being a sidekick—someone who tags along to keep the leader company. Friendships may not be totally equal, but they shouldn't center on one person.

Keep pushing for the things you want to do. If Suzanne doesn't start sharing, you can begin spending more time with somebody else. You don't have to drop her, but you don't want to waste all of your time as Suzanne's shadow.

I'm a girl and I've met this guy. There isn't anything going on between us, but we have a lot of laughs. The problem is he gets in a lot of trouble and nobody wants much to do with him. Don't you think somebody like me can help him?

Maybe. I've seen young people help young people in trouble, and I've seen the helper get hurt.

A couple of things bother me right off. If he gets into "a lot of trouble and nobody wants much to do with him," this sounds terribly serious. That makes you the Lone Ranger. If the two of you are isolated from others, I'm really concerned. I'd feel better if there were two or three people who were trying to help him. Enlist a few friends and contact an adult who can give you advice.

Alone, both of you will certainly have an effect on each other, and who can say which way that will go.

I have a friend who smokes marijuana. I don't know how to help him.

Tell him to call you when he dumps the drugs. You aren't Mr. Fixit. When things get this serious, you need to contact an adult that can help.

I have a friend who smokes marijuana. I don't know how to help him.

Can you beat this? My older sister is pregnant and my closest friend is telling everybody. I hate to drop my friend but what she has done is terrible.

There might be a better answer. Tell her how you feel. She may have thought it was common knowledge that your sister is pregnant. She may have no idea how you hurt.

All of us make mistakes. We don't have to drop friends for that.

I've seen young people help young people in trouble, and I've seen the helper get hurt.

lying, cheating, and stealing

Almost everyone in my class cheats sometimes. I don't think I can keep up unless I cheat some, too.

You are at a real disadvantage. All kinds of people are cheating, and it makes you feel like a dope if you don't. But you have to decide if some things are more important, like character and values.

Every day the news tells us about a football player, a stockbroker, a minister, a policeman, or a teacher who was caught cheating. That news is confusing to all of us. And we know that most cheaters are never caught.

Each person has to decide if he wants to be honest with himself, with others, and with God. If you choose honesty, life can be a little harder sometimes, but you will feel much cleaner about yourself and you'll please God.

> *Instead, you yourselves cheat and do wrong,*
> *and you do this to your brothers.*
> I Corinthians 6:8

Tammy copies her homework every morning from a friend of mine and hands it in. Should I tell the teacher?

No. It would be foolish to get involved in every wrong you see. Choose your battles carefully. This sounds like a problem your teacher needs to handle; let her figure this one out.

Turning cheaters in is more the work of adults than of children, and even adults must do it carefully.

Almost everyone in my class cheats sometimes.

Mark lies all the time. Even when he could tell the truth he would rather lie. Should I tell him I know he is lying to me?

Yes. Mark needs to know. He may be fooling himself into thinking that no one knows when he lies. You can do yourself and Mark a favor by telling him the truth.

My father tells me things that aren't true. He isn't kidding and I don't trust him.

Trust is like a fine vase; once it's broken it is hard to put back together. But it can be done. The first place to go is to your mother. Tell her what is happening. (She probably already knows.) Maybe your mother can talk to your father and ask him to straighten up. If possible the three of you can sit down and discuss it.

Some people have a habit of lying and they need to break that habit. Others are afraid to face the truth and keep dodging it. Someone has to confront your father and explain how he is hurting your relationship. Either you tell him, have your mother tell him, or look for a third person and discuss what to do.

Do not lie to each other.
Colossians 3:9a

The guys I hang around with are stealing from the shopping mall. I've been going along with it, but I don't feel right.

The time has come to make a hard decision. Are other people going to run your life, or are you going to take charge? That isn't an easy decision to make, but you will feel better about yourself once you make it.

You already know stealing is wrong. If you continue to go along, you will probably be caught. In that case your parents will be notified and everyone will be terribly embarrassed.

If you feel comfortable talking to your parents, talk the situation over with

the time has come to make a hard decision. Are other people going to run your life, or are you going to take charge?

them. In any case, be your own person. Stealing is a big mistake which could hurt a great many people.

Why do my friends shoplift? They just throw the junk away when they get it.

Shoplifting among children is mostly a dare/courage operation. Very seldom does anyone steal anything he really needs. Either the person is trying to prove to himself or herself how brave he is, or he is trying to prove it to a group of friends.

Without even recognizing it, some kids shoplift to outwardly express anger they have inside. Or they want to get attention, particularly from their parents.

If a person refuses to shoplift, he can prove how courageous he really is.

Last year I stole a basketball from a yard down the street. Do you think I should take it back now or just throw it away?

You need to take the ball back. The best way is to walk up to the front door and hand the ball to the person who answers. (Take a parent along if you think it might help.) Tell them you are sorry and you want to give it back.

As I say, that's the best way. If you can't work that one out, tape an apology to the ball and quietly deposit it in their yard. This isn't the perfect way, but we don't very often do the perfect thing anyway.

You shall not steal.
Exodus 20:15

My dad told us he cheats on his income taxes. I wonder if I should tell someone?

I wouldn't. The moral decision is his and the penalty will be his if he is caught. There might be a few times when children should turn in their parents, but not very many.

Some kids shoplift to outwardly express anger they have inside. Or they want to get attention, particularly from their parents.

I have a library book that's a month overdue. My sister says that's stealing. I say it's just an overdue book. What do you say it is?

Take the book back.

I told my sister I would loan her my top, but I had my fingers crossed. I don't have to loan her my top, do I?

You sound too old for that junk. Answer with a straightforward yes or no, and keep your word.

Last year I stole a basketball from a yard down the street.

sometimes teasing hurts

Uncle Fred teases all the time and it hurts.

Most of us know someone who likes to tease. Teasing can be fun if it is done only once or twice and if the person being teased thinks it's funny.

Uncle Fred probably isn't trying to hurt you. He wants to impress you by joking, and it isn't working. If you will take a couple of steps, you can help yourself and Uncle Fred.

First, tell your parents. By talking about it you let off steam and better understand how you feel.

Second, you need to explain to Uncle Fred that enough is enough. You can say it kindly. Something like, "That was funny the first couple of times, but not anymore."

Most likely Uncle Fred will back off and calm down. If he doesn't, ask your parents to say something to him.

Remember, he may be a good person doing a dumb thing.

My parents tell me not to tease my friends, but they seem to like it.

Some healthy teasing does go on. If the teasing is by a friend, if it isn't mean-spirited, and if it isn't about too sensitive a subject, some "soft" teasing can be a sign of acceptance.

When you like a person, you may want to be teased by him. Some people feel left out because they aren't teased.

But remember, teasing is a risky business. Like water, it can either refresh a person or drown him. Be alert. If there is any indication that you are hurting the person you are teasing, drop it right away.

Sandra can be funny, but I get tired of her teasing all the time.

Sandra can be funny, but I get tired of her teasing all the time.

If our friend complained or whined all of the time, we would get sick of it. If he or she is sarcastic all the time, it will start to drive us nuts. Constant teasing is boring and painful to listen to.

Tell your friend to cool it, chill out, mellow out, put it on ice, or whatever phrase will get the point across. Be sure and smile when you say it, and you will probably keep your friendship. If she doesn't stop, don't plead with her to stop. Just walk away.

I have a new teacher at school, and I can't tell if he is joking or not.

When I kid my children, one side of my lip wrinkles a little. They have learned to look for that quiver before they take what I say too seriously. If they see that twitch, they know we aren't really going to spend our vacation at an art museum.

Some of us raise our voices or drop our eyebrows or even put our hands over our mouths when we are teasing. After you have been around someone for a while, you can usually pick up what his telltale sign is.

With time you will probably figure out when this teacher is joking and when he isn't. In the meantime try to hang loose.

If you never do figure him out, you might want to mention it to him in passing. Maybe just a simple, "I'm not always sure when you are joking" and walk on by. You might help the teacher since he may think that everyone knows when he is kidding.

I enjoy some teasing, but my friend Jerry does it all the time.

Jerry could have some serious problems, or he could simply not know any other way to communicate. Bring this to Jerry's attention. Tell him he teases too much, and he might find other ways to talk to you.

Teasing is a risky business. Like water, it can either refresh a person or drown him.

Angie tells me to stop teasing her about her singing. Do you think she really means it?

Yes!

I have a friend who lies and then says she was only joking.

Don't let her get away with it. For her sake and everyone else's, she has to stop playing loose with the truth. Tell her you aren't sure what she is saying. Mention it every time she clouds up the facts.

Like a madman shooting firebrands or deadly arrows is a man
who deceives his neighbor and says, "I was only joking!"
Proverbs 26:18, 19

I get teased about being short, and I don't know how to answer back.

Don't fight back. Retaliating usually results in more teasing and sometimes in hostility. Think of a friendly, clever reply and leave it at that. How about:"That's me" or "You must be jealous."

If people see that it bothers you, they often increase the insults. Relax and roll with the punches and most people will soon get tired of saying it. They can then go and pick on someone else.

That may be the easy part. The real question is what do you say to yourself. The more you enjoy yourself the way you are, the happier you will be. Concentrate on your strengths. You are a good friend. You are a good student. You care about the underprivileged. Don't become obsessed with one or two areas about yourself. The most important part is what kind of person you are. Character is at the top of that list.

Once you feel comfortable with yourself—your nose, your hair, your chin, or whatever—he more likely you are to be comfortable with others. If you don't like short people, you have a tough problem.

In most cases you can draw your own lines and still keep a friendship. Often your good example will influence your friends in a positive way.

Some of my friends give me a hard time if I don't stick around and listen to dirty jokes. I don't like them, and most of them aren't funny anyway.

The real question is how can you not be a part of something your friends are doing without getting everybody else upset at you. The answer is "very carefully."

First, keep a sense of humor. If you walk away from a joke, say something like "too hot for me" and say it lightly. I've seen young people do that without coming across as super holy.

Second, fit in where you can. Play ball with those same people. Invite them over. Join in on projects. If you have nothing to do with them, you lose friends and become miserable.

In most cases you can draw your own lines and still keep a friendship. Often your good example will influence your friends in a positive way, and they may find more productive things to talk about. If not, you might have to get some new friends.

My clothes aren't expensive or new. A couple of people at school have started teasing me about them.

Go for your strengths. Make sure your clothes are clean and reasonably neat. If you have to help your parents with that, be sure and volunteer. Control what you can about your clothes without going nuts over it.

Emphasize your other good qualities like honesty and kindness. None of us has everything. Remember that clothes do not make the person.

You can't get rid of all the cruel teasers in the world. They are going to be around and they are going to hurt. Smart people learn not to let teasing get them down.

Some of my friends give me a hard time if I don't stick around and listen to dirty jokes.

prejudice is painful

Sometimes I wish my skin were another color. It seems unfair that I have to be put down because of my race.

Prejudice is so widespread that many of us are prejudiced against ourselves. If we are white and wish we had a South American's skin or we are Asian and wish we were white or we are black and wish we were brown, we think our skin color isn't good enough. When we don't like ourselves, we are saying the racists are right—there *is* something wrong with us.

We are also saying that God made a mistake. God does not make mistakes! He doesn't judge one color differently, and everyone stands on equal ground as far as He is concerned.

Too often grade school children go through a period when they dream of being another color. Tell that dream to get lost.

Every skin color is good. Each of us should be proud of our appearance. Our skin color is not better than anyone else's, but it is as good as anyone else's. If you cop out and hate your skin color, you are becoming a racist. Each of us has a great skin color.

Where does prejudice come from?

Prejudice comes from a variety of places:

- our relatives
- our friends
- our fears
- our books
- our schools
- our churches
- our movies
- our community

And yet, maybe none of these contributed to our prejudices. Some of it comes from outside influences and some from the choices we make as individuals.

The word prejudice means "to pre-judge." This means we either dislike or like someone before we even get to know him. Almost all of us have some sort of prejudice.

Sometimes I wish my skin were another color.

Maybe we don't like people who drive old cars, or we think rich people are snotty. Sometimes we have to talk to ourselves about our prejudices. We have to learn to give people a chance. Until we get to know someone well we aren't sure what he is like.

A smart man told me, "You will like most people if you get to know them."

> *Then Peter began to speak: "I now realize how true it is that God does not show favoritism but accepts men from every nation who fear him and do what is right."*
> *Acts 10:34, 35*

What about telling racial or ethnic jokes?

Some jokes of this nature are very funny. We should admit that. But, it is true that racial, ethnic, and religious jokes can do a great amount of harm. We would be better off if we didn't tell this type of joke about other people.

However, there is another problem. Sometimes we take ourselves too seriously.

We need to be able to laugh at ourselves. I like to joke about the glasses I wear, the bald spot on my head, some of the crazy things that go on where I go to church.

We might be better off if we told jokes about our own race, our own nationality, and our own religion. If we become too uptight, our lives are always tense. We could hurt people by telling jokes about them. We might help ourselves by laughing at who we are and what we do.

I feel put down because I am a girl.

This must be one of the biggest prejudices in the world. In most countries women are still treated as less important than men. Women have only been able to vote in the United States since 1920.

Each of us should be proud of our appearance. Our skin color is not better than anyone else's, but it is as good as anyone else's.

49

Progress is being made. As many as 40% of the classes in medical school and law school are now made up of females. As the balance shifts in the professions, men should be less likely to look down on women.

Jesus Christ was a great defender of women. He included them in His group of believers, spent time with them, and shared some of His best teaching especially with women.

Girls are equal but different from boys. They are equal in that God loves everyone the same; they are different in that they may have different strengths and abilities than boys.

There is neither Jew nor Greek, slave nor free,
male nor female, for you are all one in Christ Jesus.
Galatians 3:28

What about the people who don't speak English?

That's exactly how many of our ancestors came to this country. They came from places all over the world and most of them had trouble saying the "th" in English or they couldn't read the local newspapers.

They weren't sent home because they couldn't speak the language. They worked and learned and helped build a terrific nation.

If we know someone who doesn't speak English, we could make a deal with him. We will teach that person some English if he will teach us some of his language.

If we dislike someone merely because he doesn't speak our language, we are showing tremendous prejudice.

My church teaches that the people who attend another church are not Christians.

Here's how to find out if someone is a Christian or not: ask him. If he says he is a Christian, ask him what that means. If the person believes in Jesus

We can't say an entire building full of people are this or that. When we talk to people, we get closer to finding out what they are really like.

Christ as his Savior and proves that by attempting to follow Christ, he probably is a Christian.

We can't say an entire building full of people are this or that. When we talk to people, we get closer to finding out what they are really like.

What if someone belongs to another religion? How do we treat them then?

We love them.

I feel funny when I'm around handicapped people.

Crutches, wheelchairs, and twisted bodies make most of us feel awkward unless we are around them more often. If we get to know a person, we see more than just the handicap. There is a real person who is worth knowing if we don't let our fears scare us away.

People who are physically handicapped usually know things we don't. Blind people have learned to understand parts of life that many of us do not yet appreciate.

Once we get over the first introduction, we will discover that most handicapped people are just like everyone else.

The Lord does not look at the things man looks at. Man looks at the outward appearance, but the Lord looks at the heart.
I Samuel 16:7b

I feel funny when I'm around handicapped people.

My parents don't want me to play with the boy down the street because he is black.

When I was in grade school a black boy moved into our neighborhood. We struck up a fast friendship. After we had played together for two days, my mother said I could no longer see him because of his race.

I was totally confused. *What could possibly be wrong with playing with a person of another race?* I wondered.

If he and I had been left alone, we would have gotten along as well as any other couple of children. I still feel badly that someone interrupted our friendship.

Ask your parents what the problem is. You deserve a straightforward answer. Think over what they have to say. Politely tell them how you feel. When you have the freedom to act, do what you think is right.

I'd like to be a class officer, but I know I never will because I'm Vietnamese.

Who says you can't be a class officer? As the other students get to know you, they will probably change their minds. Hang in there. All over the country minorities are finding their way to the top.

The president of my high school junior class was from a racial minority. The president of my senior class was from another racial minority.

Minorities may have a strike against them, but many are making it.

Kids tell some awful stories that aren't true at all about a Mexican family in our neighborhood.

Don't defend them every chance you get. If a bunch of guys are telling crude stories about Mexicans, don't feel you need to jump in every time and straighten them out. Jesus Christ told us not to cast pearls before swine, and I think this is what He meant.

But, in a calm conversation, with one or two friends, feel free to correct the misinformation, and only then if you know what the facts are. It is possible to hurt people by defending them in the wrong way.

Shouting matches don't accomplish much. In some cases the thing to do is leave until you can discuss the issue when things have cooled down. But the best thing to do is to get to know the Mexican family yourself.

Shouting matches don't accomplish much. In some cases the thing to do is leave until you can discuss the issue when things have cooled down.

saying yes and no

Rhonda invites me to attend her church, but it's different from my church and I don't want to go.

You don't have to go. Feel free. Relax. But you might want to reconsider for a couple of reasons. First, that church seems important to Rhonda, and if she's your friend you need to share some experiences. Second, attendance at her church could be educational, so why not give it a shot?

Don't go with her if your parents object.

I want to be Larry's friend, but he wants me to join a special club and I don't want to.

Turn Larry down but give it your best tone. Tell Larry thank you for the invitation (you can say that sincerely because you realize how much the group means to him). Then tell him the society isn't for you, but you prize his friendship anyway.

Never be rude to a kind and generous offer.

Cindy's always trying to borrow money from me, but she doesn't pay it back. How do I tell her no next time?

Say, "I can't lend you money because you don't pay it back," or just say, "I can't lend you money anymore." You don't have to explain.

What do I do when my friends ask if they can copy my homework?

Tell them you can't do that. Your friends will understand, and your enemies don't count.

I hate to turn anyone down about anything. I'm afraid they won't like me.

If you say yes to everything, you will be misused and people will not respect you.

What do I do when my friends ask if they can copy my homework?

When you need to say no, be polite, be definite, and be firm. The first person you want to respect is yourself. Respect is more important than like.

Amy always wants me to visit her grandmother in the nursing home, and I don't know how to turn her down.

Why not say yes? A few minutes in a nursing home would probably be good for Amy, her grandmother, and you. Amy isn't asking you to rent a room there, just to spend a few minutes.

When I go to this guy's house after school, he always offers me a beer out of his dad's refrigerator. I never know what to say.

Just say, "No, thanks," and stick with it. Alcohol can be a disaster at your age. For the next few years, one person or other is always going to be pushing a beer in your face.

You need to make a decision and not let the peer pressure drive you crazy.

I have this group of friends who go to the store after school and look at centerfolds in magazines. I don't want to go, but I don't want to tell them why.

Frankly, I don't think you have to tell them why. Who says you have to make a speech? Simply slip away in another direction. If you are asked why, say, "I'm not going with you today." You can say no without explaining. We become boring if we step up on a soapbox and deliver a lecture every time we don't agree.

This girl at school says she'll do my homework if I'll be her boyfriend. What do you think?

She must really think you're dumb. You better file her under history.

Just say, "No, thanks," and stick with it. Alcohol can be a disaster at your age.

strange and evil thoughts

My brother is so mean that sometimes I really want to hurt him, and I mean really hurt him.

So far you're in good shape. We're all capable of thinking mean and cruel thoughts. Now you need to do something before you start planning to carry those out into actions.

Let your parents know how much it bothers you. If they aren't available, look up a school counselor or an extra good teacher.

Sounds like you need to let off steam before you're tempted to go too far. After you let off steam, you need to get some suggestions on how to get along better with your brother.

It seems like I'm always down on myself. Most of the time I think about the things I can't do well.

Try a mental workout program. Make your brain jog a little. Do some mental push-ups.

What are a few of your good qualities? Are you a dependable friend? Are you thoughtful? What school subject are you pretty good at? What do you do that your parents appreciate? Do you treat your grandmother, your aunt, your school bus driver well?

When you concentrate on your strengths, you make them stronger. If you keep repeating what you think are weaknesses, they become the most important part of your life. Try to think of ways to turn your weaknesses into strengths.

Grab a pair of mental barbells and get to work Every time your mind begins to sag, go over your strengths again. Then add a few.

Too many of us spend all of our time working out on put-downs. Spend more energy on push-ups and put-ups.

I thought about taking money from my parents' drawer, but so far I haven't.

You have the right idea. Now try to think about it less.

My brother is so mean that sometimes I really want to hurt him, and I mean really hurt him.

After watching horror shows, I have nightmares. Do you think other people have dreams like that, too?

Ask your friends if the horror shows bother them. My guess is that many are afraid of dark rooms and of dreams like yours. If these shows are driving you bonkers, you would be smart to stop watching them and select more positive shows to watch.

Sometimes I think of myself as the adopted daughter of a faraway king and queen. Then I imagine that they will come and get me and take me home.

How often do you dream this? Can you control the dream, or does it reoccur without your cooperation?

Fanciful dreams or daydreams are common. We have all dreamed that we live in a mansion or own a big horse ranch or something. However, if the dreams are frequent over a long period of time and you can't control them, you could have a pressing desire to escape. In that case look for a dependable counselor and tell that person what is going on.

I often think terrible things. I would be ashamed to say what I've thought.

It's not okay, but it's okay. That is what makes it all so confusing. Horrible thoughts pass through our minds—murder, theft, cruelty, getting even, beating people up, sexual acts are just a few. There aren't many things that we can't think of. Our minds are like slide shows with plenty of pictures rattling through.

Expect all kinds of thoughts to come and go. That's perfectly normal. The trick is to keep the bad thoughts moving so they don't become ideas you want to carry out. The more we panic over our bad thoughts, the more they will come back. If this continues to be a problem, you might want to talk to an adult whom you trust.

the trick is to keep the bad thoughts moving so they don't become ideas you want to carry out.

young stress

There's this guy who is always looking for a fight. He gets right in my face and says stupid stuff. How long do I take this?

Use your head. Outthink the guy. Go around him; don't answer him back. Smile and keep your cool. Just because he is looking for a fight doesn't mean you have to give him one. Most guys like this calm down after a while, or they start looking for someone else to pick on.

It's a tense situation with no easy answer. But don't let someone else control your actions—if you can avoid it.

There's a big boy on the next block who always gives me a hard time if I go past his house. Don't tell me to stay away from his place.

I'm going to anyway. For about three years I tried fighting everybody who gave me an ugly look. It was dumb, and one fight led to another with someone else.

You don't have to stay away from his place all of the time, but I would cut down on the number of trips in that direction. If you get proud and walk close to him too often, you might be looking for a fight you can't handle.

Don't let your pride take over. You can't let everyone run you off, but smart people have enough sense to avoid trouble.

If you were walking down a street and that street became a pier, would you keep walking into the ocean? God gave you enough sense to turn to the right or to the left.

There's a big boy on the next block who always gives me a hard time if I go past his house.

Pride only breeds quarrels.
Proverbs 13:10a

I'm overloaded. How can I tell my parents that I'm under too much pressure?

Tell them what you've told me. Children today face many more pressures and stresses than your parents faced at your age. If children are yelling for help, we had better let up and let them be children.

Families with two parents must be easier than those with one parent. We seem uptight most of the time.

One-parent families certainly have some tough times, but don't assume that two parents would make life a trip to videoland. Some parents fight and argue nearly all the time. Too many parents get drunk or drugged and scream over every little thing.

The carpet isn't always greener at the neighbor's house. Over 60% of today's children will live with one parent at some time. It may be smarter to look for ways to get along with the one parent you have and thank God for him or her.

It seems like young people are shooting themselves left and right. Are more people committing suicide these days than in the past?

Suicide among young people apparently is up. But we can't be sure of that. The population is large and we keep statistics better than we used to. But it still looks like youth suicides are up.

If the increase is real, that suggests a few things. Young people may need to talk more and find release for their feelings. We also may have to take some of the pressure off and let people chill out more frequently.

Late at night I get headaches and I can't sleep. I wonder if I worry too much.

Tell your parents exactly what you told me. You might have a physical problem, and your problem might come from stress. Don't keep it to yourself. Either way, you need relief.

Children today face many more pressures and stresses than your parents faced at your age.

Sometimes I cry on my way to school. I'm afraid I can't do everything right.

There's a lot going on—schoolwork, music lessons, ball games, clubs to attend. Naturally you want to do them the best you can. But you don't sound like you're enjoying them. If you're crying very often, something has to give.

Tell your parents how you feel. Tell your school counselor. Tell them both. They may be able to show you how to relax and even laugh. You might need to drop an activity or two. You are smart to discuss it before you let the tension build too much and you burn out.

A girl on the school bus really scares me. Nobody wants to sit next to her. How can I calm down?

Start by talking to your heart. Tell your heart to relax. Almost certainly nothing is going to happen and there is nothing to gain by being anxious every day.

Second, ask Christ to show love through your face, attitude, and actions. If she sends out tension messages, be sure you are radiating peace and love.

Late at night I get headaches
and I can't sleep. I wonder if
I worry too much.

> *He gives strength to the weary*
> *and increases the power of the weak.*
> *Even youths grow tired and weary,*
> *and young men stumble and fall;*
> *but those who hope in the LORD*
> *will renew their strength.*
> *They will soar on wings like eagles;*
> *they will run and not grow weary,*
> *they will walk and not be faint.*
> *Isaiah 40:29-31*

Sandy likes to pick, pick, pick at everything I do. How can I stop her?

Ask her to stop picking on you. The next time she does it, ask her again. Then if she persists, get out of her way.

My brother Ben acts like a big clown in school. Shouldn't he take things more seriously? He gets terrible grades.

Since he clowns and has terrible grades, he could have an underlying problem of stress. Maybe Ben feels that he can't learn his schoolwork or otherwise keep up with the class. He may be hiding behind his clowning mask.

Explain your concern to your parents. They might be able to sit down with Ben and discuss what might be bothering him.

Before I take a test I get so nervous I can't think. Sometimes I think I'm going to go nuts.

You're too young to wear a straightjacket. Next time you take a test, try a few simple steps:

1. Be sure you've studied.
2. Count to ten while breathing slowly and deeply.
3. Think of something fun you will do when it's over.
4. Tell the muscles in your arms, hands, and fingers to relax. Tell them one by one.
5. Check in with God and remind yourself that the two of you will still be friends no matter how the test turns out.

Before I take a test I get so nervous I can't think.

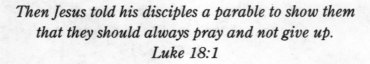

Then Jesus told his disciples a parable to show them that they should always pray and not give up.
Luke 18:1

Everytime I start to do something, my sister tells me all the reasons why I can't do it. I feel pretty good about it until she starts talking.

Tell your sister to put a sock in it.

When I watch television for awhile, I get nervous. There's nothing going on but I just get nervous.

My questions would be:
    How long is "awhile?"
    How much exercise do you get?
    You might need to see a doctor about your nervousness, but many people who watch too much television seem to get fidgety.

You might need to see a doctor about your nervousness, but many people who watch too much television seem to get fidgety.

61

someone to talk to

I need to talk to someone, but I don't know who I can trust.

None of us are sure whom we can trust until we get to know him or her. We can't sit in our rooms and expect to hear a message telling us we can trust "Mr. X."

Often the following people are your best first contacts:

- friends
- parents
- teachers
- ministers
- youth directors
- counselors
- psychologists
- youth phone lines

Get the ball rolling and see if you feel comfortable with that person. If you have a friend who would recommend someone he has talked to, that might be a good route to go. Get a conversation going and see if you feel some trust building between the two of you.

I share most of my problems with a close friend. Sometimes I wonder if that's smart.

We use friends as counselors more than any other group of listeners. Most of us soon learn who are dependable and who are bad news. Ask yourself several questions about the friends you talk to:

- Do they seem to care about you?
- Are they listeners or do they talk over you?
- Do they make suggestions or do they tell you what to do?
- Are they bossy?
- Do they tell others what you tell them?

These are just starting questions, but if you like the answers to these, you probably have a friend with whom you can share.

My friend told everybody my secret.

Tell your friend you are disappointed that she told your secret. Also, tell her

I'd like to talk to my parents, but I know they don't understand today's kids.

62

that she will have to prove she can be trusted before you will share anything important with her again. For the time being, don't share anything with her but the weather and cookie recipes.

I want to talk to my youth minister, but I already know how he feels about what I've done.

Do you know your youth pastor well enough to make that statement? He might come across differently to you if you asked his counsel away from the regular youth group meeting. If he comes across as rigid, condemning, and not helpful, you are probably wasting your time. But he may surprise you. Don't look for someone who agrees with you. That might not be the greatest, either. Find a person who listens and understands. If your youth minister isn't that friend, look somewhere else.

My friend, Angela, has all kinds of problems. I can't deal with all of them.

In a loving way decide what your limits are. Begin by controlling how much time you spend listening and which subjects you want to deal with.

After you listen for a while say, "I have to go in ten minutes, but I want to hear more about this tomorrow." Be available but don't let your friend own your life.

If the subject is something you think is too serious or too unusual for you to comprehend, say so. In a nice way say you don't know anything about that, but maybe she or he should talk to Mr. and Mrs. So and So.

I'd like to talk to my parents, but I know they don't understand today's kids.

Don't write your parents off just because they take naps and watch the evening news. Some parents are old-fashioned, close-minded thinkers. But many aren't.

Create a conversation. Tell them what it is that makes you glad and sad. You might discover that your parents are caring and make excellent listeners.

don't write your parents off just because they take naps and watch the evening news.

You can best trust a help line if a parent, teacher, or minister recommends it.

What about phone lines for young people. Are they worth calling when you have troubles?

Some seem to be run by excellent people. Often the person you talk to is well-trained and tuned in. If you call, ask right off what qualifies them as good listeners.

Encourage the big cheeses at your church to consider starting a phone line for youth. They might be surprised at who will call and what people want help with.

If your church doesn't have a phone help line, ask if your school has one. You can best trust a help line if a parent, teacher, or minister recommends it.

the alcohol problem

Don't a lot of people drink alcohol and never get drunk?

Yes.

Aren't some people more likely to become alcoholics than others? My cousin says people are born drunks.

"Born drunks" is a strong term and isn't quite accurate. Some people may be more likely to become an alcoholic than others. Whether that is because of their personality, body chemistry, or strictly their choice is still being argued. It's different with each person.

Some can handle alcohol better than others. The problem gets worse when a person thinks he can handle anything.

Why do adults always make speeches against drinking? They know kids are going to drink sometime.

Adults know that some kids start drinking early and get "hooked" before they know what hit them. Others kids get in car accidents and lose their licenses. Still others drink and hurt themselves or hurt others. The adults are trying to help kids decide not to drink before they get into situations that are hard to handle.

And by the way, it is illegal for kids to drink in most states until they are 18 or 21.

Some of my friends are drinking already. The stuff smells terrible. Why do they want to drink?

The number one reason is peer pressure. That's what almost every young person tells me. They don't want to be different and they don't want to be left out. How many people have you heard say "I just love the taste"? Not many young people say that.

Some of my friends are drinking already. The stuff smells terrible. Why do they want to drink?

If adults tell us not to drink but they drink, aren't they just being hypocrites?

Some are, and some aren't. But don't use that as an excuse for doing something dumb. Wouldn't you be better off making the smart decision to hold off deciding whether or not to drink until after you finish school? Then you can evaluate the situation and won't have hindered your brain development in the meantime.

Alcohol isn't really the problem anymore. The real trouble is in drugs. Knocking alcohol is old-fashioned.

Drugs are often the most talked about problem, but alcohol abuse remains a huge destroyer of young people. Teenagers are still wrapping cars around trees, still drinking themselves unconscious, and still becoming alcoholics. It's true that drugs are getting the most attention, but alcohol is doing amazing damage—some of which lasts a lifetime.

My friends don't seem to be serious drinkers; they just like to play drinking games.

Some of the drinking games result in the most serious drinking. Often young people will drink two or three times as much beer if they are playing a game. This may be especially true of girls. In games where the winner gets to choose who has to down the drink, girls are most often selected. Before long they are drinking far more alcohol than they expected.

Nothing much will happen if you keep count of how much beer you drink and stop.

There are a couple of problems with that theory. First, you don't know how much a few drinks have affected you. Many drunk drivers thought they had everything under control.

Second, the problem is that you lose count. After a couple of drinks many young people can't tell how many they have had. Drinking runs away from us in a hurry.

If alcohol is so bad, why don't they outlaw it?

They aren't going to outlaw alcohol, and if they did people would be making it in their basements. The better solution is to get control of ourselves.

Trying to scare us out of drinking doesn't work. Young people will leave it alone only if they want to.

Absolutely correct. Every young person has to look in the mirror and ask what he wants out of life.

It looks like drinking is fun. What's wrong with wanting to have fun?

Nothing is wrong with wanting to have fun. The trick is finding a way to have fun that doesn't hurt you or anyone else.

How much alcohol does it take to get drunk?

That depends on what you are drinking and what your size is. It also may depend on your body chemistry, what you've eaten, and how tired you are.

Everyone wants to be popular, and if it takes alcohol to be popular, I guess we are going to do it.

That's exactly the name of the game. But if some leaders in the school have enough courage not to drink, they could help turn this around.

I wish my parents would transfer me to a Christian school. I think I could resist alcohol better there.

Maybe you could and maybe not. You can get alcohol anywhere if you want to get it. The decision will always be yours to make.

I wish my parents would transfer me to a Christian school. I think I could resist alcohol better there.

Wine is a mocker and beer a brawler;
whoever is led astray by them is not wise.
Proverbs 20:1

what are drugs like?

Isn't it true that Coca Cola® used to have cocaine in it?

A hundred years ago cocaine was promoted as a cure for all kinds of ailments. Psychiatrists recommended it, pharmaceutical companies sold it, and soda fountains mixed it with syrup. Coca Cola® was one of the many companies which used cocaine.

After more was learned about how dangerous cocaine was, it was removed from soft drinks in 1906.

If you use drugs, what do they do to you?

Users report various types of effects. Drugs can work both to stimulate and to depress. A person might become more alert, have added energy, be sexually charged, find new courage to mix socially, and feel high. A high or a buzz is like feeling picked up or perky.

Some drugs depress appetite and cause people to lose weight. Some drugs make you see and hear things that aren't really there. But, remember that all supposed pluses become negatives with long and increased use.

How can drugs hurt you?

Too many ways to mention here.

Number one is addiction. Addiction means you develop a strong, irresistible craving for the drug and feel you must have it. You are then hooked like a fish on a line.

Number two is financial. Increased use of drugs is terribly expensive. Frequently the addicted person must rob, steal, and cheat to come up with enough money to support the habit.

Number three is side effects—stomach problems, loss of sleep, sex problems, anxiety, fear, irritability, and on and on and on. The physical problems it creates by high blood pressure and even convulsions after use over a long period of time, can also create long-range problems that do not go away.

If you use drugs, what do they do to you?

Can drugs kill us?

Absolutely. The abuse of drugs can kill, especially people who have some illnesses or who mix the drug with other substances. Sometimes it's hard to tell how much you are actually getting. You may take too much by mistake. Recently the use of dirty needles used in shooting up drugs has been found to spread fatal diseases such as AIDS.

> *Do you not know that your body is a temple of the Holy Spirit, who is in you, whom you have received from God? You are not your own; you were bought at a price. Therefore honor God with your body.*
> *I Corinthians 6:19, 20*

What other kinds of drugs are there besides cocaine?

There are plenty of destructive and addictive drugs and there always will be. LSD, heroine, crack, and marijuana are only a few, and there are people trying to create new drugs. These people are looking for a new high and a way to make lots of money.

We will never be able to get rid of all drugs. Some victims get high from medicines they buy at the local drugstore. The only answer is: don't start using them.

If a person is addicted to a drug, can he be cured?

The drug user must want help. If he or she does, there are programs available. To help an abuser who doesn't want help is extremely difficult.

But many young people have accepted Christ into their lives and have been set free from drugs. They receive the Holy Spirit, have guidance from God, and have a reason to be alive. Christ gives them the strength to give up drugs. He has rescued thousands.

Many young people have accepted Christ into their lives and have been set free from drugs.

If you have cocaine and intend to distribute the drug, you could possibly get 15 years in prison. One court has ruled that this includes giving cocaine to your friends.

Is it illegal to have cocaine if you don't use it?

Laws can change, but the present information I have makes it a federal crime to simply possess cocaine. The penalty can be up to one year in prison and a $5,000 fine. Most states have a similar law.

If you have cocaine and intend to distribute the drug, you could possibly get 15 years in prison. One court has ruled that this includes giving cocaine to your friends.

Many states have laws against possessing drug paraphernalia. Those are the snorting straws, cutting devices, and weighing equipment for cocaine use.

How do people take cocaine?

There are four popular ways to take this drug:

1. Snort it up your nose.
2. Swallow it.
3. Freebase or smoke it.
4. Inject or shoot it into your body.

Isn't cocaine usually used by street people and crooks?

Not so. Some studies indicate it is most often used by high school and college graduates who are holding down a job. However, as they become addicted they create a huge need for cash so they can buy more drugs. The need for money then turns some into thieves and sellers of cocaine.

getting in touch with school

getting along with teachers

My math teacher has the personality of a toad.

Don't pay any attention to her or his personality. If the teacher sends out bad vibes, you send back the best feelings you can. Learn math for one year and move on to the next teacher.

Personality clashes between teachers and students almost always end up hurting the student. Chill out and don't let the teacher rattle you. Your teacher next year might be the best in the school.

Everybody knows my teacher has it in for me. You can just hear it in her voice. Anything I do just makes it worse.

You're in a tough fix. Tell yourself a couple of great principles:

1. You will try to love people who aren't easy to love.
2. You will not do battle with a teacher.
3. You may need to forgive her often.
4. Play it cool and move on next year.

Those are attitude checks. Don't let an unfair teacher make you become mean.

If the situation is so bad you think you must take action, here are some suggestions:

1. Go to the teacher and say, "I'm sorry I did that; I hope you aren't angry about it."
2. Talk to your school counselor, principal, or another teacher.
3. Ask your parents for suggestions.

Don't go to war over every little thing a teacher does. If you do, you will be fighting for years. Most teachers get over their student problems after a short time.

My math teacher has the personality of a toad.

Some of the kids give me a hard time because one of the teachers gives me a lot of breaks. What am I supposed to do, tell her to quit being so nice?

So what's wrong with a teacher giving a student an extra break or two? The best situation would be for the teacher to give everyone a break, but you can't control that very well.

There are some pitfalls to avoid. Don't butter up or flatter your teacher. Don't start "playing" for her favor above anyone else's. That kind of behavior makes our friends want to barf.

At the same time, be civil, polite, considerate, and friendly to your teacher. Everyone should treat her that way. If she doesn't treat all students the same, that's her problem. All you can control is your behavior, not the teacher's.

If you stay fair, most of your friends will understand if the teacher gives you an extra break. Teachers usually treat someone a little bit better than they do others.

I have a teacher who attends my church. At school I call him by his last name but at church I want to call him "Don." Is that alright?

Ask him.

I'm afraid they will put me in Mr. Anderson's class next year. I can't convince my parents to call the school and keep me out of there.

Did you take a piece of paper and write out all of your reasons? That way you make sure you have all of your best reasons together. If your parents still are not convinced, then you might not have a strong enough case.

Give Mr. Anderson a try. Look for as many good things as you can find. We all have to get along with people, and some of them are cranky characters. If you do find the situation unbearable, you can go back to your parents and try again. But in almost all cases it works out okay.

Personality clashes between teachers and students almost always end up hurting the student. Chill out and don't let the teacher rattle you.

My soccer coach screams every time I make a mistake. If he keeps it up, I want to quit the team.

Some coaches are screamers and others are calm teachers. Personally I think the screamers overdo it, but there are plenty of those around.

Quitting doesn't usually solve much. A better approach might be to simply accept the coach for the way he is and don't take it personally.

Some coaches attack what the player did. Other coaches attack the player and call him or her stupid or lazy or worse. The ones who attack the player are the ones who really hurt.

Let him yell and scream. You know life doesn't rise or fall over a soccer game.

How much do I have to take from a teacher?

That's a broad question. One measuring stick is this: if the teacher continuously belittles you, calls you names, or insults you, make an appointment with the school counselor or principal, or tell your parents. Teachers might make mistakes, but no teacher has any business tearing a student down.

This may not seem like a problem, but I have a terrific teacher and I don't know how to tell her without sounding like an airhead.

It isn't easy to be kind. Start off with a simple, direct, "Good job!" or:

You made that clear.

Your classes are interesting.

We learned a lot today.

You don't have to get terribly mushy but a sincere compliment is appreciated by anyone. Give it a shot.

Our teachers get mad if we pass notes in class. Isn't that a dumb rule?

No.

My soccer coach screams every time I make a mistake.

My teacher is always throwing out her opinion, but if I give my opinion she cuts me off. That isn't fair, is it?

No, it isn't fair but that's the way it is. Sometimes we have to accept situations which aren't fair.

I have a crush on my fifth-grade teacher. I think about him all the time. That's scary.

It doesn't have to be. Your feelings are normal and probably will pass soon. You may always think he is good looking, but next year you may find yourself daydreaming about another teacher. You sound like a healthy fifth grader. Don't let it frighten you.

Every day we knock the teachers while we eat lunch at our table. Sometimes I feel dirty about it.

Normal grousing about teachers is harmless. But day-after-day complaining is ugly and can make you feel cheap. Don't make any big speeches about the evils of teacher bashing, but when you can, change the subject to television, sports, or video games.

Normal grousing about teachers is harmless. But day after day complaining is ugly and can make you feel cheap.

sports pressure

After losing a basketball game, we got on the bus to go home and were kidding around. The coach came on the bus and chewed us out. He said, "What do you think this is, a game?"

This will get me in trouble with some coaches, but I think it ought to be "just a game," especially in grade school and junior high. There is too much pressure too soon on young people.

That's why intramural sports is such a great idea. Let the kids play against each other without parents there to watch. Let games be games.

I'm not much of an athlete, and I hate to participate.

I'm not much of an athlete, and I hate to participate.

It's tough, but if you can manage, keep your sense of humor. First, go ahead and play, but remember if you drop a ball, that's really a small part of life, even though it's hard at the time.

Second, not all of us develop at the same rate. A few years from now your coordination may improve and you might find a sport you love.

Third, aim for a sport you enjoy now. You don't have to play baseball or be a football star. Do you like to run or play tennis or climb mountains or lift weights?

Try a wide variety of sports and you might find a couple you enjoy. The best purposes for sports are fun and recreation. We don't have to beat everyone in order to feel important.

*For physical training is of some value, but godliness
has value for all things, holding promise for both
the present life and the life to come.*
I Timothy 4:8

The boys in my school who are good at sports act like they're hot stuff. Shouldn't someone set them straight?

The problem here isn't sports. You will find students with good grades who act like they're hot stuff, too. Cheerleaders, chess players, artists, singers, and banjo players are all capable of looking down their noses at others. Some excellent athletes are also great people.

Whenever they choose sides for a ball game, I get picked last. You would think I'd get used to it but it still bothers me.

Sports is high pressure. So many of us can't relax and simply enjoy a game. Winning is too important. As long as we are so competitive, people are going to get picked last. The same is true in the classroom.

Keep this in mind when you get to do the selecting, whether it's for a quiz team, a math team, or whatever. Mix it up. Give everyone a chance. Don't forget how you felt and try to be kind to others. Meanwhile a sense of humor is your best route to go.

I press on toward the goal to win the prize
for which God has called me heavenward in Christ Jesus.
Philippians 3:14

I'm a girl. We play ball on Saturdays, but I can catch and hit better than the boys. They all call me a "tomboy."

Don't worry about what they call you. No girl should hide her athletic ability because the boys can't keep up. Be polite, don't rub it in, but give sports your best.

I don't like physical education class. I want my mom to write a note and get me out of it.

Why? If you give up on sports this early in life, you may never know what you

aim for a sport you enjoy now. You don't have to play baseball or be a football star.

might have enjoyed. Gym class may not be your favorite, it might even be painful, but you really need to stick in there.

I like to play Ping-Pong, but that means I either win or lose. Either way we don't play much more because neither one of us likes to keep losing.

Don't stop playing because you fear losing. You can't avoid that risk in any game you play. Let your loss challenge you to try harder.

You can also try playing doubles. It's lots of laughs and everyone seems to want to keep playing.

In Little League football I'm a tackle. I feel like I must be stupid to play the line.

You aren't stupid. If you enjoy playing the line, why not do it? Some of the smartest people I've met grew up knocking heads in football uniforms.

My Little League coach likes to chew us out when we make mistakes. I told my dad I want to quit.

You are going to get chewed out by someone no matter what you do. The music teacher, the bus driver, the janitor can all yell at you about something. The best step is usually to hang in there and get used to doing things under pressure.

In Little League football I'm a tackle. I feel like I must be stupid to play the line.

Everyone who competes in the games goes into strict training. They do it to get a crown that will not last; but we do it to get a crown that will last forever.
I Corinthians 9:25

We have a pool table and my dad always beats me. I don't like to play, but he gets upset if I don't.

The age difference between you and your father suggests that you should not be in competition. One way to keep playing is for you to stop competing with him. Set your own goal regardless of what your dad does. Try to put five balls in the pockets before he clears the table. If you get five balls, you have done well.

Compete with yourself—at least until you get as good as your father. Tell him what you're doing if you want—that might cut the tension.

Our teacher comes out at lunch and runs the ball games. He always puts his favorites at bat or in the best positions. What can I do about it?

Not much. Anything you do will probably make it worse. Try to give your best to the game and let your talents speak for themselves. You might even be on his pick list for the next game.

Compete with yourself—at least until you get as good as your father.

how important are grades?

My parents are always on my case about grades. How do I get them to back off?

Get better grades.

I think everybody puts too much emphasis on grades.

You're probably right. But since so much importance is placed on report cards, you can't afford to ignore grades.

Try a couple of guidelines:

1. Make learning your goal, and grades will take care of themselves.
2. Get good enough grades to keep your options open. You don't want to find out later that you can't get into the school you want because you got a "Z" in biology.

You may think grades are dumb, but right now there isn't much you can do about it. The best thing is to keep them respectable.

My parents think I should get all A's and B's. I tell them I can't do that well.

How do you know? Go to the school counselor or the principal and ask what kind of grades you could get. I bet you'd be surprised.

One of my teachers says grades are a lousy way to teach children. I agree with her.

She may be perfectly correct. But grades help us know what we've achieved, how we compare with others in a subject, and how much help we still need. They also provide a goal. Don't be afraid to try because you feel you might fail. Risk taking is important.

You can't afford to totally blow grades off. Keep them respectable. Presently, it is a way to measure achievement.

I think everybody puts too much emphasis on grades.

In the meantime, here's an idea. Sit down with a couple of your friends and think of a better system than grades. Then take the idea to your teacher and explain the program. Maybe it could be for a class assignment. If you present your approach well, you might be able to make a change and feel a part of the solution.

My parents ground me if my grades go down. Is that fair?

It's fair if that's the way they choose to do it. Parents have different ways of showing concern. They are looking for a method that might motivate you to live up to your potential.

The best solution is to work harder on your schoolwork, and then you won't have to sweat the grounding.

It's okay for my parents to scream about my grades, but they never show me what kind of grades they got in school.

What would that change? They want you to do well in school whether they did well or not. They might show you their report cards, but that still won't get you off the hook.

If the teachers think you are a C student, they keep on giving you C's.

That does happen, but not with all teachers. They do seem to be influenced by neatness. Write as clearly as you can, and they are likely to notice the improvement. Also, be sure your work is completed on time. If a teacher sees added effort and better-looking work, he may think you have gotten smarter.

Also, it doesn't hurt to ask a teacher what you can do to get better grades. If done sincerely, most teachers are more than willing to help you achieve your goal.

It doesn't hurt to ask a teacher what you can do to get better grades.

The teacher grades my art-work. I say you shouldn't grade creative stuff.

The teacher grades my artwork. I say you shouldn't grade creative stuff.

It's difficult to grade creativity. You can't grade creativity as you would a math assignment. But the teacher *can* grade effort. Did the student try? Did he spend time and energy?

The concept of "grading" seems to kill creativity. So give it all you've got in the effort department and see what happens to your grade.

I think the pressure to get good grades starts too soon.

It really depends on the student. Some kids are challenged by the competitiveness; others are shy and don't want to be pushed. We all learn in different ways, but we only have one system for all types of learners. One possible solution might be not to give grades during the first four years of school. The teacher could note your progress and discuss it with you privately.

Don't look for a big change anytime soon.

getting in touch with my sexuality

awkward boys

When does a boy's body start to grow up?

Sometimes as early as ten years old, but usually he starts to mature at eleven or twelve. He may continue to change into his early twenties.

What kind of changes should I expect?

These things will happen during puberty, but not necessarily in this order:
Hair growth on your face, genitals and under your arms.
Muscles start growing.
Your voice deepens.
Your penis and scrotum (balls) grow larger.

What is puberty?

Puberty is the time when your body takes on mature sexual characteristics, and you begin to become capable of producing children.

I'm twelve years old and haven't changed like my friends have.

People grow at their own rates. Some will begin slowly while others could have a first moustache at eleven. Often they will have growth spurts and one summer will grow several inches.

If things don't seem to be happening as quickly as you expected, don't worry. Your body will change, probably in the not too distant future.

I'm afraid I'll grow up short. I'm behind everyone else now. How can I know?

You can't know for certain, but here is the guideline. If both of your parents are short, you may well grow up to be short. If both of your parents are tall, you may well grow up to be tall. If you have one short parent and one tall one, you could go either way.

I'm afraid I'll grow up short. I'm behind everyone else now.

But because of good nutrition and healthy bodies there are exceptions to these guidelines.

I seem to be knocking things over and tripping. I'm afraid I'm going to break things.

When your body begins to grow rapidly, it doesn't grow evenly. Your arms may be longer and you might have trouble getting use to their new range. It happens to everyone for a while but things will even out.

Other boys are getting hair under their arms and between their legs and I'm not. Is there something I'm supposed to do?

Keep busy and don't sweat it. Your body hair might arrive late, but that often happens. You might not get chest hair or heavy hair on your arms or legs, especially if you are fair-skinned.

Remember, hair doesn't make you a man, character does.

My voice is getting higher instead of lower.

Voices do funny things while they are changing. Yours will probably drop as you grow. At least it will come under control.

Voices do funny things while they are changing. Yours will probably drop as you grow. At least it will come under control.

growing girls

Help! What are all these body changes that are supposed to happen to me?

These are the basic changes and roughly the order in which they will happen:

Breasts begin to enlarge.

Hair appears between legs (genital areas).

Menstrual cycle starts (called periods). Ask your parents for a good book on menstrual cycles.

Hair grows on legs and underarms.

Hips start to widen.

Glands produce more oil resulting in acne and stringy hair.

Don't panic if some of these changes arrive slowly or if one happens before the other.

I praise you because I am fearfully and wonderfully made.
Psalm 139:14a

What is puberty?

The time when your body takes on mature sexual characteristics, and you begin to become capable of producing children.

Why is puberty so hard?

It seems hard because of the rapid changes, both physically and socially.

Why are boys so immature?

Don't be too hard on the guys. They mature more slowly than girls but will catch up later. Boys also feel a need to be aggressive, especially when it comes to sexual subjects. They are more likely to say words that will shock girls. Boys

What are all these body changes that are supposed to happen to me?

often will tease girls about breasts or sanitary pads or anything else they think might embarrass the young ladies.

My mom and I are always arguing over what I should do. She treats me like a kid.

Your mother is almost as confused as you are. As your body grows, you are sort of halfway between. You are on a bridge crossing over from childhood to adulthood. That makes you part child and part not.

Be patient with your mother as she tries to figure out how quickly you are making this transition.

If I want large breasts, is there an exercise I can do or some foods I should eat?

Breast size isn't as important as some people pretend. Teenage boys act like they are hypnotized by size, but as they grow up they realize that the real person is more important. Being kind, loving, and caring is what really counts.

I have no idea how to enlarge breasts.

You are on a bridge crossing over from childhood to adulthood. That makes you part child and part not.

what is love?

Am I too young to be in love?

Not at all. You love your parents, your friends, and possibly you love God. You may be too young to commit yourself to love a person in a romantic way, but you're capable of love.

My parents fight most of the time, and I don't think they love each other anymore.

That's hard to know. Love takes work. If we don't take care of it, love can die out. But don't judge your parents. Only they know how much love they have for each other.

What's the difference between love and sex?

Sex is something you do. Sex can be an event like boxing, a warm bath, a good swim. But above all, when you have a special feeling of love for someone (which we call being "in love") and you marry that person, sex is an important way to show that person a very special kind of love. It's so special that it's worth waiting for.

Love is the way we care about a person. Love wants to help, to share, to be involved.

If we love a person we may marry him and have sex with him. But too often people have sex with someone they don't love.

If we feel very strongly that we want to have sex with someone, that doesn't necessarily mean we love him. Sex can be just an exciting thing to do. But this is something that God intended for two people who commit to each other for a lifetime in marriage.

What's the difference between love and sex?

When someone on television has sex, he says he made love. It must be the same.

No. All we know is that they had sex. You can have sex without making love. People have sex with people they don't even know.

> *And now these three remain: faith, hope and love.*
> *But the greatest of these is love.*
> *I Corinthians 13:13*

I'm afraid I'll fall in love when I don't want to or I'm not ready.

Love is an amazingly strong force. But you are stronger than love if you want to be. You may meet a person whom you could fall in love with, like a meteorite crashing to the ground. But you can put the brakes on if you want to. It might be tough, but you can do it.

Here are some suggestions to help you:
1. Control your daydreams. Try to think about other things.
2. Watch how much time you spend with that person. Plan a variety of activities that keep you involved with a group of kids rather than only one person.
3. Avoid intimate touching like fondling and heavy kissing. The more involved you get with a person, the harder it is to slow down the relationship.

Save your love and give it to the person you choose. It's like a dart. Wait until you are ready, then aim carefully and hit the bull's-eye.

You may meet a person whom you could fall in love with, like a meteorite crashing to the ground. But you can put the brakes on if you want to.

why wait to have sex?

What do people do on dates? Do we have to have sex or what? I'm afraid to start dating.

You can date often and not have sex. If your date insists you have sex, get away and call your parents.

Is it all right if I have sex before I get married?

There are three answers to that:
1. NO!
2. NO!
3. NO!

What's wrong with a dating couple having sex?

Look at the facts:
1. You can get pregnant. Ask the millions who have abortions if you can get pregnant.
2. You can get diseases. Sexually transmitted diseases are on the increase. These diseases can disfigure and kill. People who reserve sex for marriage do not get sexually transmitted diseases.
3. The Bible tells us to run away from all kinds of immorality (I Corinthians 6: 18-20). Our bodies weren't created to be used in the wrong way.

My friends say you can't get a date unless you are willing to have sex.

With some guys you can't. Don't date those guys.

Isn't there a double standard? How come boys can have sex but girls aren't supposed to?

There should be only one standard. Wait until you get married so no one will get hurt.

What do people do on dates?

If you're smart and careful, you won't get pregnant.

Every pregnant girl I ever met believed that statement.

Adults just don't want us to have fun.

Maybe some adults are against fun. But getting pregnant or diseased isn't fun. It also isn't any fun to have a guy use you and then drop you.

I'm too young for all this sex talk. I'd rather wait until I'm older to discuss it.

That makes sense, except for this: don't buy a lock for your front door after the house has been robbed. It's terribly painful to give sex education to pregnant girls and unwed fathers.

Where can we go on dates?

Since you don't have cars, your range will be limited.

Don't be in a hurry to date, but when you do date, try to stay active and keep it light. Mall dates are fun in some localities. Skating, bowling, or just going out for snacks are good choices. Stay away from movies that center on sex and could put unnecessary pressure on a date.

Church youth activities are good places to take dates. Games, picnics, rallies, music concerts are excellent. But again, don't be in a hurry.

don't be in a hurry to date, but when you do date, try to stay active and keep it light.

the AIDS problem

AIDS sounds horrible, but what is it?
It stands for Acquired Immune Deficiency.

    The reason someone has this deficiency is because he received a virus called Human Immunodeficiency Virus, commonly called HIV.

What does AIDS do?
The virus attacks the body's immune system leaving the person an easy victim to infections and cancers. Since the body cannot fight these illnesses and diseases, the person often dies.

How do we get AIDS?
Presently there are four known ways to get AIDS:

1. Having sexual intercourse with someone who has the HIV virus. The virus can be transmitted between heterosexuals (men and women) or homosexuals (men and men or women and women).
2. Using an intravenous drug needle or syringe which an infected person has used. (These are needles that enter the veins.)
3. Receiving contaminated blood products usually during a blood transfusion.
4. Being born to a woman with AIDS. (And sometimes from breast-feeding.)

Can you get AIDS by mosquito bites?

Can you get AIDS by mosquito bites?
The four ways listed above are the only ways a person can get AIDS.

    You cannot get the virus by:

- shaking hands
- sneezing
- water fountains
- toilets
- coughing
- breathing
- food service
- mosquitoes

- or being in the same house, school, church, office, factory, or any other place with a person with AIDS.

Does everyone with AIDS die?

It's too early to say if everyone dies, but most people do pass away. However, medical cures are being worked on as we write this book.

Do more homosexuals or heterosexuals have AIDS?

So far the number of homosexual victims with AIDS is vastly greater than the number of heterosexual victims. The goal is to stop it from spreading among both groups.

Is there some way for couples to be sure they don't receive AIDS by having sex?

There is one absolute, totally safe method. If a couple gets married without having sex before marriage, and then they never have sex with anyone else but their marriage partner, that couple will never get AIDS by having sex.

Sex can be an enjoyable experience without the fear of AIDS if a married couple is faithful to each other all their lives.

Can a person get AIDS by giving blood?

No!

Can a person get AIDS by getting blood?

There is still a slight chance but only if a mistake is made. Blood is now checked for the virus and not used if it flunks the test.

What do most people with AIDS die from?

Pneumonia and cancer.

How can you tell if someone has AIDS?

Most of us can't. For a long time people with AIDS look like everyone else.

Could a person have AIDS and not know it?

Yes. It could take eight to ten years for the disease to show itself.

If a couple gets married without having sex before marriage, and then they never have sex with anyone else but their marriage partner, that couple will never get AIDS by having sex.

How should we treat people who have AIDS?

With care, love, and compassion!

Before long most of us may know some family which is directly affected by AIDS. I know of several families already.

AIDS victims are in churches, schools, factories, and hospitals. We should act toward them as we would anyone with an extremely serious illness.

Can you get AIDS from having sex only one time?

Yes!

How does AIDS pass from one person to another?

There are only two known ways: it passes through blood or through semen.

How can a child get AIDS?

Through any of the four ways we mentioned earlier. Some children need regular blood transfusions and received the HIV virus before thorough blood checks were made.

Can a person in school get AIDS from a student?

No. Not if he does not contact internally that persons blood or semen.

Will there ever be a medicine to cure AIDS?

Anything is possible. What will probably happen is a medicine will be discovered which will hold it in check. The illness will remain but its affects will not be as devastating because the virus has been treated.

What other diseases can you get from sex?

As with AIDS, if a married couple never has had sex with anyone but their marriage partner, it is practically impossible to get a sex related disease.

Some of the other diseases around are gonorrhea, syphilis chlamydia and genital herpes. They can be extremely dangerous and in some cases can kill.

AIDS victims are in churches, schools, factories, and hospitals. We should act toward them as we would anyone with an extremely serious illness.

could we be homosexual?

I'd rather be with other girls than be with boys. Is there any chance I'm gay?

Not on the basis of that evidence. As you grow older you may find that your interest in boys might grow. There isn't anything wrong with wanting to be with people of your own gender.

What makes a person gay?

I should get a prize if I can answer this one. Let me explain the two major possibilities:

1. A person might be born with a physical or chemical makeup which makes him want people of his own sex.
2. A person makes a decision to be gay. A young man finds he enjoys the company of other men better than he enjoys females. Or a female enjoys other females more than males.

There is probably some truth to both of these and also some nontruth.

Being gay or lesbian doesn't refer to liking someone of the same sex. Gay or lesbian means someone continuously likes to have sex with a person of the same sex. One experiment or adventure with sex does not mean the person is gay or lesbian. God's original plan was for men and women to have sex with people of the opposite sex.

I am a boy and I like to cook. Some of my friends call me gay.

Some of the best cooks in the world are men. Girls who play softball are not gay and neither are boys who sew. Our interests in life do not determine if we are gay or straight (term used for someone who is not a homosexual).

I am a boy and I like to cook. Some of my friends call me gay.

That isn't how Jesus Christ would treat people and neither should we. If he is gay, he should be accepted like any other human being.

There is a boy at school who people say is gay. The other boys like to beat on him.

That isn't how Jesus Christ would treat people and neither should we. If he is gay, he should be accepted like any other human being.

If I shower with other boys I find myself looking at their bodies. I don't know why I do that.

Probably because you're curious.

Patty says my girlfriend and I are gay because we like to sleep together. That isn't true.

Tell Patty to go take a nap.

There are two women who live together on my street. Everybody says they must be gay.

Our imaginations are going nuts. It's okay for two people of the same sex to live together in the same house. It's alright for a person to remain single all his life. A person's life-style doesn't mean she's gay.

96

is the good feeling really bad?

Sex feels like a good idea now. Why do I feel dirty when I think about it?

There's no need to feel dirty. Your body is maturing exactly the way God wanted it to mature. Feel happy about the good feeling, but save sex for marriage. Like all good experiences, it needs to be protected.

What is masturbation?

When someone stimulates himself or herself sexually.

Sometimes I want sex very badly.

You will probably have this feeling from time to time most of your life. If everything goes according to plan, you will eventually get married and the two of you can have sex together.

Do girls masturbate too, or just boys?

Both boys and girls masturbate, but not every person chooses to masturbate.

I heard you can tell if a person masturbates because his face breaks out with pimples.

Years ago lots of people believed that statement. It's not true. You also don't lose your hair, grow hair on your hands, or go blind.

What causes wet dreams?

Sometimes a boy will have an erection of his penis while he is sleeping and will release semen. When he wakes up, he will find a wet spot on his clothes or on the sheets. This is a normal release and shouldn't worry the boy. In technical terms this is called a nocturnal emission. Nocturnal means nighttime.

Sex feels like a good idea now. Why do I feel dirty when I think about it?

I've started to think about girls most of the time. Am I oversexed?

You sound normal to me.

How do you know if your penis is big enough?

Penis size is a worry among many boys but it needn't be. Length and size is seldom a problem. Almost certainly you are growing at an average rate.

Do boys have to go through something like a period? Why do girls have to get this?

Boys don't experience anything quite like a menstrual period. Sometimes girls don't think that's fair, but a period is necessary as part of the baby-producing process.

    Many girls feel upset that boys don't get a period. God simply didn't bless boys with the ability to have children.

When will boys grow up and stop making sex jokes?

Many never stop.

Why do boys tease girls about their breasts and periods?

Boys feel awkward, nervous, and a little confused by their body changes. Much of their crudeness is an attempt to get used to their own sexual growth.

    Did you ever have a new haircut and feel embarrassed about it? Boys feel that way about sex but much more so.

How can you tell what your breast size will be.

You probably can't. Relax as best you can. Breast size doesn't turn a girl into a woman. Boys put a lot of emphasis on size, but that has nothing to do with the person you are.

    If a girl worries too much about breast size, she can get her values upside down.

Do boys have to go through something like a period? Why do girls have to get this?

Don't girls mature faster than boys?

Definitely. But boys catch up later. At least I think we do.

Do girls have breasts just to feed babies?

Breast-feeding is one major purpose; another is part of the sex play with their husbands.

How do people have sexual intercourse?

A girl receives a boy's penis in her vagina which is between her legs. If the couple does not use some kind of protection, she can become pregnant. Even if they use birth control, it is still possible to become pregnant. There is no absolutely, totally safe way to guarantee that she cannot get pregnant if she has sex.

> *Flee from sexual immorality.*
> *I Corinthians 6:18a*

Can you get pregnant the first time you have sex?

Yes.

Sex sounds like too much trouble.

Sex is powerful. It can create a huge amount of pleasure and good. That same sex can cause harm and heartache. It is much like water, which can be just what you need but can also drown you. Almost everything which is good has a downside if it isn't controlled.

How is a baby made?

A sperm from a male's penis enters through a female's vagina and attaches to an egg. This is called conception. The fertilized egg then implants itself to the uterine wall inside the female.

there is no absolutely, totally safe way to guarantee that she cannot get pregnant if she has sex.

getting in touch with difficult things in my life

what is death like?

When my mother died, did she become an angel?

God already has plenty of angels. Besides, if God wanted more angels, He could create them. God did not take your mother because He was short on angels. In fact, God probably did not take your mother.

We die when our bodies stop working. God may have welcomed your mother into heaven when her body quit, but that doesn't mean He "took" her.

They put my grandfather's body in a grave. How could he still be alive?

The part of us that continues to live is called our soul or our spirit. It's like having your personality stay alive after your body stops living.

It helps me to think that my father's smile and kindness are still alive. I don't know what form his personality has or exactly where it is today, but his soul has not died.

Is there a heaven?

The Bible tells us there is a heaven. I don't know where it is or what the furniture looks like. The Bible teaches that God is there.

When we put our faith in Jesus Christ, our names are written in heaven and we are citizens of heaven. Our human bodies are flimsy like tents. When we die we receive a permanent place to live in heaven.

What is it like to die?

> *Now we know that if the earthly tent we live in is*
> *destroyed, we have a building from God, an eternal*
> *house in heaven, not built by human hands.*
> *II Corinthians 5:1*

death is a scary subject. But often we can remove much of the fear if we find someone to talk to about it.

What is it like to die?

I don't really know. However, I have watched people die, and at the time they seemed eager to move out of this life into another one.

Do pets go to heaven?

I hope so. Some pets mean so much to children and adults that they would love to see them again in the next life. Unfortunately the Bible gives us no reason to believe that pets go to heaven. It probably is true that pets are meant to be enjoyed only in this life. Maybe we will have to wait and see.

Will our bodies come back to life?

There is a time in the future when bodies will be resurrected. They may not look exactly like our present bodies, but they are probably similar.

It is sown a natural body, it is raised a spiritual body.
I Corinthians 15:44

Why didn't God stop my father from dying?

I don't know. Maybe that is something you will want to discuss with God in heaven.

This doesn't mean I don't care. I could guess, but I would probably be wrong. Someday God will remove all death, but why He doesn't do that today is a question I cannot answer.

My mother died last year. What will happen to me if my father dies, too?

That's a good question. It's unlikely that your father will die anytime soon, but the thought does occur to you. The person to answer this is your father. Don't be afraid to bring up the subject; he will probably be glad you did.

You will feel better if you can discuss some of the possibilities. Would you move in with an aunt and uncle or with a grandparent? Who would you be comfortable with? Tell your father how you feel.

I hear people say, "Only the good die young." Is that true?

No. It is only a saying that we throw around without much thought. We also say, "He's too ornery to die."

You can go ahead and be good; you won't die early.

My cousin, Brenda, died and I don't really feel very bad about it. Is there something wrong with me?

We don't all feel the same way. If you don't feel bad, there is no sense in pretending. Be polite and respect the feelings of others, but you don't need to fake a feeling you don't really have.

I prayed that my grandfather wouldn't die. But he died anyway. What did I do wrong?

It sounds to me that you did the right thing. You asked God to heal your grandfather. That seemed like a good idea. For some reason God did not intervene and keep your grandfather from dying.

There is no harm in asking. A good God must have had a reason for not saying yes at that moment.

Do pets go to heaven?

I am afraid that I am going to die. I try not to think about it, but the fear doesn't go away.

Do you have any idea why you are afraid to die? Have you recently seen a relative or a pet die? Have you seen something on television which makes you feel you are about to die?

Death is a scary subject. But often we can remove much of the fear if we find someone to talk to about it. Pick out a good listener like a minister, a schoolteacher, a school counselor, a parent, a grandparent, someone whom you respect and would enjoy talking to. If that person can't help you, he probably can recommend another person who can help.

Part of the reason Jesus Christ died on the cross was to free us from the terrible fear of death. Let someone help you handle that fear.

> *And free those who all their lives were*
> *held in slavery by their fear of death.*
> *Hebrews 2:15*

Do people always die when they have cancer? My grandmother has cancer.

Millions have had cancer and after treatment have gone on to live many years. Cancer can kill but often it doesn't. Early treatment is important.

Take the time to get close to your grandmother. You might want to write, call, or visit her. Be optimistic and make your time together fun and special. She could be with you for many years to come.

My uncle died recently, and I don't know what to say to my mother.

You don't have to say much. Maybe something simple like, "I miss Uncle Larry, too," or "This really hurts." The best help you might give is to be a good listener. Let your mother talk and express her feelings.

It means a great deal to have someone nearby who cares how we feel. You don't have to quiz her. Often you can sit alone silently. If she asks to be alone for a little while, you can come back later.

Other things to say are:

I love you.

Can I sit with you?

Uncle Larry was a good guy.

Part of the reason Jesus Christ died on the cross was to free us from the terrible fear of death.

It wasn't fair that Aunt Jean should die so young.

I agree; it wasn't fair. Maybe God would agree, too. God likes to see us with the people we love. He must feel hurt that we have to be separated.

When God makes everything right, there will be no more death and no more crying and no more pain.

> *He will wipe every tear from their eyes. There will*
> *be no more death or mourning or crying or*
> *pain, for the old order of things has passed away.*
> *Revelation 21:4*

The minister said my grandfather was in heaven, but they put his body in the ground.

Your grandfather's soul or spirit or personality has left its body. The spiritual part of Grandfather is the part that went to heaven.

Will I ever see my father again?

Everyone who believes in Jesus Christ as their Savior has been promised an eternity with Him. There will be a great meeting place where we will gather.

I miss Aunt Lou so much I often cry. I don't want to go to school or anything. I don't think I'll ever smile again.

She must have been very special if you miss her this much. The pain or hurt may last a long time. But what usually happens is that the good memories begin to move the pain out of the way. You may always miss her, but hopefully you will soon be able to smile at those memories instead of cry over them.

Talk to friends and relatives. Tell them the stories of how much she meant and means to you. Those memories are too good to keep to yourself. As you share the stories, the happy times will rush to the surface and make you even more thankful for when she was around.

I miss Aunt Lou so much I often cry. I don't want to go to school or anything.

You need to express your grief in your way and others have to do what helps them.

How come a lot of people don't even care that Uncle David died? They act like nothing happened.

Everyone has to deal with death in his or her own way. Someone may miss him tremendously and yet not cry at all. Another person might think the best way to handle his death is to keep working.

You need to express your grief in your way and others have to do what helps them.

Everybody is so busy, no one has time to be with me.

Tell someone exactly that. They may think you are getting along great. Often adults feel awkward talking to children, but if you say something first, they might open up. Pick out someone you like and trust. Tell him or her what you said here.

when serious illness comes

Why does God allow good people to get sick?

There is no easy quick answer for this one. As long as there is evil in the world, people will get sick. Someday God will remove all evil and there will be no more viruses or bacteria or cancer cells or weak heart arteries. Until then God continues to love every sick person and invites them to become part of his family.

My mother is in a wheelchair and will never walk again. What if I pray and ask God to give her new legs?

Do it right now. Tell God how you feel and what you want. Miracles do happen and there are people up and walking who used to be confined to wheelchairs. But realize that God may not remove the chair. In that case, look for ways to enjoy your mother in a wheelchair.

What are some of the places you can go with her? What are some of the games you can play? What are some of the jobs you can do together around the house and in the yard?

My guess is that she doesn't want everyone to sit around feeling sorry for her. Get together and take the biggest bite out of life that you can take.

The doctor says I have a heart condition and have to be careful what I do. I get depressed thinking about how short tomorrow might be.

It's one day at a time. For all of your problems you have learned something that most of us forget. Today might be our only day. I had better give it my best shot because I could be out of here tomorrow.

Depression is a hard one to fight. Some of us are in the habit of giving in to it. You sound like you are determined to keep your spirits high. Maybe if you

My mother is in a wheelchair and will never walk again.

can find another person to care about, that might help give you an extra purpose as you grab hold of each day.

We need to learn from you. Let me know how you handle this tough one.

Do not boast about tomorrow, for you do
not know what a day may bring forth.
Proverbs 27:1

Some people don't like to be asked about their illness because they feel like they are being quizzed.

Bobby has leukemia. I want to know how I can help, but I don't know what to say.

Hang around. Treat Bobby like anybody else and wait for him to open up. Some people don't like to be asked about their illness because they feel like they are being quizzed. Give him time and space. When he wants you to know, he'll say so.

Once a month my dad goes to the doctor. When he comes home he and my mother whisper the rest of the day. I'd like to know what is going on.

Ask them a direct question, "How is Dad anyway?" It's important that you be able to trust them and they trust you. There might be some things they won't want to share with you, but they must make that decision.

Let them know you care and want to be part of whatever is going on.

the miserable life of runaways

My parents are ridiculous. Sometimes I want to run away.

Think twice before you run away and then don't do it. Life on the streets is a total, horrible disaster.

Reach out to someone and ask for help—school counselors, ministers, youth workers, teachers—they are your key contacts. There are alternatives to running away, and they can help you find them.

I don't think I can stand it here anymore. I've got to make plans to leave.

Plans is the key word. If the situation is oppressive, painful, and hopeless, you have to make that decision. But don't just jump out. Go to someone and explain your problem. Try a counselor, a policeman, a minister, a teacher, a grandparent. Don't leave home alone. Look for help.

How do kids live on the street?

Their first two problems are something to eat and some place to sleep. Usually children are too young to work so they steal. If stealing doesn't work for them, some kids sell themselves to men or women for sex.

The streets are a constant, desperate battle. Children hide from the police on one side; they are abused by adults and drug dealers on the other. It isn't a cute life of roaming around on a beach eating coconuts and bananas. This is a miserable world of danger, pain, fear, hunger, cold, loneliness, and drugs.

How do kids live on the street?

What I have thought about doing is to run away for just about a month. When I come back, my parents would treat me a lot better.

When you come back you will be a changed person (if you make it back).

most of us think about running away. Even adults are tempted to catch a bus and head for someplace.

Think of thirty days scrounging for food, sleeping in abandoned buildings or under bridges. Think of creepy people who like to hurt children. Try to imagine being scared almost to death.

If there is something you want to change, you'd be better off changing it at home.

Sometimes I get angry and want to leave home. The feeling always goes away, but I wonder if sometime I'm going to just do it.

Most of us think about running away. Even adults are tempted to catch a bus and head for someplace. We would like to change our circumstances or change the pressures we face.

It sounds like your home life has always improved enough for you to be able to handle it. You have good bounce. You get down, but you snap back. Remember that. You have plenty of reason to expect a bright tomorrow.

Bobby and I have talked about running away together. Wouldn't we be pretty safe if it's the two of us?

There is bravery in partners, but there's also foolishness. Your odds aren't improved much at all. Children are often stolen, smuggled across borders, and murdered. The fact that there are two of you could make you a better catch for some pervert.

Sorry. There isn't much good to be said about running away.

getting in touch with God

what is God like?

Is God a man or a woman?

Neither one! God is a spirit (John 4:24) and can't be male or female. We often think of God as having white hair and a long beard, but this is just our imagination.

Since God doesn't have a body or hormones or muscles or body parts, God cannot be a man or a woman.

God is called a "he" regularly in the Bible because we have a language problem. We can't call God "it" because God is a person. God is a person who is a spirit—not a person who has a human body.

What does God look like?

A spirit doesn't look like a human being. I don't know what God looks like and I may never know.

Is God just the wind or something?

The wind cannot think, love, or create alligators. God is more than merely a force. God can plan ahead, figure out solutions to problems, answer prayers, and talk to people.

Certainly the wind has a force which is superior to ours, but God is much more than a force. God has feelings, and He can be moved to sadness and happiness.

What does God look like?

In his distress he sought the favor of the LORD his God and humbled himself greatly before the God of his fathers. And when he prayed to him, the Lord was moved by his entreaty and listened to his plea.
II Chronicles 33:12, 13

Does God have a hand?

The Bible uses the word *hand* but not in the same way we use it. The *hand* of God can send a storm or send clouds, but that wasn't really a hand. What it means is that God did something. By using the word hand we can better picture what God was doing.

God acts but He doesn't really have a hand or a finger or a foot.

Does God get angry?

The Bible tells us about the anger of God. Anger can be a natural and even necessary emotion. Try to remember a few things about God when He gets angry:

1. God gets angry at evil like war and starving children and murder and abuse. He isn't just a hothead who flies off the handle throwing a fit whenever He wants to.
2. Anger isn't God's normal emotion. He doesn't spend all day grouchy and grumbling. But there are things that bother Him.
3. In the New Testament the love God shows in Jesus Christ is emphasized far more than His anger.
4. There is nothing wrong with a God who gets upset over evil.
5. God isn't a moody monster who is out to get us. God is love and He always cares about us.

How can God be everywhere at once?

There is nothing and no one exactly like God. He is unique. Only God can be present in all places all of the time. We say He is *omnipresent*. Even air which is found almost everywhere on earth is limited, but God is not limited. He can be everywhere at the same time and still care about your cold and sore throat.

Heavy stuff.

God is not limited. He can be everywhere at the same time and still care about your cold and sore throat.

No one has ever seen God; but if we love one another,
God lives in us and his love is made complete in us.
I John 4:12

God doesn't toss us out because we fail. We are too special to Him for that. God knows that we sin and He loves us anyway.

Who made God?

Almost everything you and I see has a beginning and an end. Seeds become trees and after many years they die. Cars are manufactured. Pictures are drawn and colored. Pets are born, live, and die.

God doesn't have to fit into any of these groups. God has a quality called eternal. He has neither a beginning nor an end.

We haven't seen anything that has existed forever. But God simply always was and always will be. He is not limited by time.

Sometimes I doubt there is a God.

Most of us doubt there is a God sometimes. That doesn't mean there is anything wrong with you, and it doesn't mean there is no God.

Some days you don't feel well or you read about a terrible accident where ten children were killed and you wonder why God didn't do something to stop it. God understands that doubt happens, and He still loves us.

The next day most of us bounce back and choose to believe there is a God.

"If you can'?" said Jesus. "Everything is possible for him who believes." Immediately the boy's father exclaimed, "I do believe; help me overcome my unbelief!"
Mark 9:23, 24

How can I believe in God more than I do?

Put two things to work: your imagination and the Bible. If the Bible says Jesus walked on water, children seem to have an easy time picturing that. They can imagine Jesus taking short steps or long strides. Can you imagine Jesus splashing water with the sole of His right foot and laughing?

But some adults get uptight about it. They want to know if there were rocks under the water or if it was really a beach at high tide.

Children are great believers because they are not afraid to use their imaginations. Can you picture the disciples taking a few loaves of bread and feeding thousands of people? No problem. Children can picture the disciples handing out fish sandwiches all day long.

Keep your imagination loose and you can see things you haven't seen yet.

> *Though you have not seen him, you love him; and even*
> *though you do not see him now, you believe in him.*
> *I Peter 1:8*

Why doesn't God stop people from getting divorced?

That seems like a great idea. If God is God, He can do anything. He could put His finger on a mother's and father's heart and cause them to love each other. But by doing so He would take their choices away. God wants us to love each other because we want to. We don't love people simply because we have to love them.

We are free to make decisions. God doesn't want to remove that freedom—even if it hurts.

I mess up a lot even when I try to do what's right. He must get tired of me failing so much.

Fortunately God has an inexhaustible supply of understanding. All of us mess up. We do it accidently and we do it on purpose. God understands that. It's like having an old bike. If the tire goes flat, you fix it. If the handlebar grip wears out, you replace it. When the seat tears, you either patch it or get a new one. But you keep working with the bike because it's special to you.

When we mess up, God gives us His forgiveness. He gives us patience. He adds a little love. He throws in His kindness. God doesn't toss us out because we fail. We are too special to Him for that. God knows that we sin and He loves us anyway.

How can I believe in God more than I do?

But God demonstrates his own love for us in this:
While we were still sinners, Christ died for us.
Romans 5:8

What kind of music does God listen to?

God hears all kinds, but the kind He enjoys is a little harder to answer.

I don't like to call God my father. My real father is sort of mean and I don't really trust him. Do I have to call God, Father?

Why not address God as Friend or some other title given for God in the Bible? Many people have had a difficult time with their real or biological father, and they are uncomfortable thinking of God in the same way.

None of us are perfect fathers. Some of us dislike our fathers for a few years and like them again later. A few never care much for their dads.

Don't let a name or a title get in your way. Pick a word you like and one you think God would appreciate. The most important part is to talk to God, not what you call Him.

Oh, for the days when I was in my prime,
when God's intimate friendship blessed my house.
Job 29:4

Does God care about everything I do?

Yes. However, I'm not sure God cares whether you ate peanut butter today. I don't think God is style-conscious and hates to see you wear blue socks with tan trousers. God isn't a nitpicker worried over how you comb your hair.

But God definitely cares about you as a person and about the things in your life. He cares about how you respond to others and how you handle circumstances that come your way. God cares about life and death, about love and

I think of God watching over me. He knows when I'm in trouble. He knows when I'm happy. This is a comfort to me. It makes me feel safe.

hate, about forgiveness and revenge. If we hurt someone or someone hurts us, He would be concerned. God cares about the important things.

Cast all your anxiety on him because he cares for you.
I Peter 5:7

Can God see everything I do?

God is able to do anything He chooses. If He wants to watch me brush my teeth or cut my toenails, God has the ability to do that. But frankly, I don't picture God staring at me every minute of the day and night. If I think of God as always looking at me, wide eyed, I could go nuts.

Instead I think of God watching over me. He knows when I'm in trouble. He knows when I'm happy. This is a comfort to me. It makes me feel safe. He also knows when I've been up to no good. And knowing this can help remind me not to sin when I get into a tough situation.

There is a huge difference between watching over us and staring at us. If a parent takes a three-year-old child to the playground, the parent keeps an eye on that child, but the child is free to run and climb and explore. The parent is there, but he doesn't sit and stare in the child's ear.

God watches me and gives me the freedom to roam around. Too many kids are frightened because they imagine that God is staring over their shoulder watching their every move. Relax. God doesn't want to drive you nuts. He wants you to feel safe and loved.

Does God care about everything I do?

117

am I a Christian?

I go to church and all that, but sometimes I have my doubts about it all.

Doubt isn't entirely bad. Most of us have it from time to time. The good thing is that doubt makes us reevaluate what we believe and come back stronger than ever. Don't try to doubt; that's asking for trouble. But when doubt comes, look at it as an opportunity to strengthen your faith.

How can I know I am a Christian?

There is a way to be certain. The basic plan is this: tell God you are a sinner and you would like to change. Ask Him to forgive your sins and come into your life. Then begin to follow Jesus Christ, using the Bible to guide you along the way.

For additional information, talk to your minister.

Stories like Jonah and the fish bother me.

Stories like Jonah and the fish bother me. Do I have to believe them to be a Christian?

Jesus Christ, His life, death, and resurrection are the real issues to concentrate on here. Putting a personal faith in Him as your Savior determines whether or not you are a true Christian.

You might want to check Matthew 12:39-41. Jesus made a clear reference to the story of Jonah. Obviously He believed it.

My Sunday school teacher said if we were truly Christians we wouldn't watch so much television.

I can't find that in the Bible. However a biblical principle saying we need to think about good things is in the Bible. It is always a good idea to evaluate what you're watching on TV and make sure it is building you up and not just filling your mind with garbage.

Finally, brothers, whatever is true, whatever is noble, whatever is right, whatever is pure, whatever is lovely, whatever is admirable —if anything is excellent or praiseworthy—think about such things.
Philippians 4:8

I am a Christian but church bores me every Sunday. Does that mean I'm not spiritual?

Not necessarily. Most churches are aimed at adults and not at children. The vocabulary, the music, and the message whistle over the heads of most people your age.

Tell an adult that you would like a children's sermon or a children's church or something that hits you in your world.

Last week I lied to my mother. Now I am afraid I'm not a Christian after all.

Christians foul up. We do dumb things, make mistakes, and sin. Tell your mother you're sorry. Ask God to forgive you and try to clean up your act. But you are a Christian on the basis of your belief in Jesus Christ, not on the basis of your behavior.

I'm a Christian, but I'm not really that good. Sometimes I think I act like everybody else.

Often we do act like everybody else. Some days I'm very good and other days I'm a hair ball. God understands that, and He wants to see more days when I'm very good.

But how good I am isn't what makes me a Christian. We are Christians because we accept what Jesus Christ did in dying for our sins. He paid for the days when I'm a hair ball.

We all have bad days, but God is willing to keep working with us.

How good I am isn't what makes me a Christian. We are Christians because we accept what Jesus Christ did in dying for our sins. He paid for the days when I'm a hair ball.

We all need to ask God to help us to carry out the good we would like to do. With His help we might be surprised how much we can do.

I tell myself I'm not going to sin, but I don't hold out for long. Why do I keep doing things that are wrong?

Did someone tell you that if you became a Christian you would do everything right from then on?

Sin goes with life. We continue to make mistakes and do things that we know are wrong. The neat thing is that we can ask God for forgiveness and ask Him to help us do better. Each day can begin with a clean slate. Relax and try to aim for the things we know are good.

When I think of Mother Teresa or someone like that, I know I can never be that good of a Christian.

If you look at other Christians and envy them, you can get depressed. Be you. Be strong, tough, loving, helpful you. That's who God wants you to be. Don't get confused trying to be someone else.

I dream about all these people I want to help. I picture myself being friends to the poor and teaching people to read and all that stuff. But I don't really get much of it done.

There was a great apostle who had the same problem you have. He wanted to do good things but he kept messing up: *For I have the desire to do what is good, but I cannot carry it out. For what I do is not the good I want to do; no, the evil I do not want to do—this I keep on doing* (Paul in Romans 7:18b, 19).

We all need to ask God to help us to carry out the good we would like to do. With His help we might be surprised how much we can do.

For God so loved the world that he gave his one and only Son,
that whoever believes in him shall not perish but have eternal life.
John 3:16

talking to God

I want to pray but I don't know what to say.

How do you talk to your friends? God isn't looking for any special words. There is no strange way you have to address Him. You don't have to call Him "Sir" or "Your Highness."

If you want, you can call Him "Father" and then simply tell God what you are thinking. Are you thankful? Is there something you want? Do you have some questions? Are you simply looking for a chance to chat?

God is a great listener. He would simply like to hear whatever is on your mind.

Everytime I start to pray, I think God must have more important things to do than listen to me. When's the best time to call Him?

Talk about a communication system? God can take all incoming calls at once. He can handle the most complicated questions and problems without missing a detail.

Many of us feel like we don't want to bother God until we realize His capabilities. Just punch the button anytime for instant access.

I've asked God for something special, but He hasn't given it to me. I thought He answers prayers.

He does answer prayers, and for some reason He has decided not to grant this request, at least not yet. God may have reasons which you can't begin to understand.

God has the right to answer no or wait awhile. Tell Him again how you feel. The situation might change and God will decide to help you with it.

When's the best time to call Him?

> *Is any one of you in trouble? He should pray.*
> *Is anyone happy? Let him sing songs of praise.*
> *James 5:13*

If I asked God to close the school down for a day, would He do it?

Remember that God is interested in building character, not in providing for your every wish. He knows your motive for asking, and He also knows what works for everyone's best interest. Be careful what you ask Him for. He might convince the school board to start having school on Saturdays.

What if I ask God to quiet my brother down? He is always embarrassing me.

Give it a try if you want. A better way might be to ask God to help you handle your brother's noisiness without getting so upset yourself.

> *So I say to you: Ask and it will be given to you; seek and you will find; knock and the door will be opened to you. For everyone who asks receives; he who seeks finds; and to him who knocks, the door will be opened.*
> *Luke 11:9, 10*

My dad prays before we eat supper and he prays forever. Isn't there a way to get him to shorten it?

No problem! You volunteer to pray.

Do I have to close my eyes when I pray?

If you keep your eyes open, can you concentrate? God doesn't tell us to close our eyes. You can stare up at the sky or look at the floor if you want. The question is how can you best think about what you're doing?

We have this kid who prays before he eats a hot dog. Isn't that too much?

We'll leave that up to him.

If I asked God to close the school down for a day, would He do it?

What good is the Lord's Prayer if we just repeat it every Sunday?

That depends on the person. Reciting the prayer can be extremely meaningful for some. Others can't get into it and should pray their own way. Whatever turns your propeller.

When I try to pray I always feel like a creep. I can't imagine why God would want to listen to me.

But He does. That's the miracle of it all. We don't have to have it all together before we can talk to God. He doesn't think we're creeps. We aren't perfect but God knows that. Still He invites us to come to Him on a one-to-one accepting basis.

Jesus Christ promised that He would never run us off: *All that the Father gives me will come to me, and whoever comes to me I will never drive away (John 6:37).*

God is very accepting. He isn't nearly as hard on us as we are on ourselves.

We aren't perfect, but God knows that. Still He invites us to come to Him on a one-to-one accepting basis.

getting in touch with the future

future world

Is nuclear war coming?

It's less likely today than it has been for the past fifty years. Superpowers like the Soviet Union and the United States seem presently more interested in cutting back on their military, and European countries are more concerned about cooperating and taking care of their own problems. Tensions can change quickly, but for now things look good.

Will Jesus Christ return?

He promised He would come back and Christians expect Him to. Christians differ a great deal over how and when He will return, so it's best if you ask your minister for the details.

Will we all suffer a lot in the future?

Be an optimist! Nobody knows exactly what tomorrow holds. But since we trust in Jesus Christ, we know we can let Him take care of it.

The Bible speaks of periods of intense persecution. It also describes many years of peace. As a Christian I look forward to the years of peace, but I also know the agony could come.

"Men of Galilee," they said, "why do you stand here looking into the sky? This same Jesus, who has been taken from you into heaven, will come back in the same way you have seen him go into heaven."
Acts 1:11

Will Jesus Christ return?

Could Jesus Christ return today?

If it fits God's plan, Christ could return anytime.

I'll let God worry about tomorrow, and I'll take it one day at a time.

Behold, I am coming soon! My reward is with me, and I will give to everyone according to what he has done.
Revelation 22: 12

A minister said everything is going to burn up anyway and he expects worldwide war in a few years. If that's so, why do I want to finish school?

Who knows what's going to happen tomorrow? Anything could. God expects me to make the most of my life. I'll let God worry about tomorrow, and I'll take it one day at a time.

this is really the beginning

We would have a great deal to worry about if we didn't place all of our tomorrows into God's hands. All of our cares become easier if we trust our unseen heavenly Father to watch over and take care of us. Smart Christians look to God for guidance and help.